WITHDRAWN

410

YORK HANDBOOKS

GENERAL EDITOR:
Professor A.N. Jeffares
(*University of Stirling*)

e last date shown below.

AN INTRODU
TO
LINGUISTICS

Loreto Todd
MA (BELFAST) MA PH D (LEEDS)
*Senior Lecturer in English,
University of Leeds*

LONGMAN
YORK PRESS

D0231197

YORK PRESS
Immeuble Esseily, Place Riad Solh, Beirut

PEARSON EDUCATION LIMITED
Edinburgh Gate, Harlow,
Essex CM20 2JE, England
Associated companies, branches and representatives
throughout the world

First published 1987
Eleventh impression 2000

ISBN 0-582-79293-2

Produced by Pearson Education Asia Pte Ltd
Printed in Singapore (B & Jo)

Contents

Chapter 1

What is linguistics?

LINGUISTICS IS USUALLY DEFINED as 'the scientific study of language'. Such a statement, however, raises two further questions: what do we mean by 'scientific'? and what do we mean by 'language'? The first one can be answered relatively easily but the second needs to be examined more fully. When we say that a linguist aims to be scientific, we mean that he attempts to study language in much the same way as a scientist studies physics or chemistry, that is systematically, and as far as possible without prejudice. It means observing language use, forming hypotheses about it, testing these hypotheses and then refining them on the basis of the evidence collected. To get a simplified idea of what is meant, consider the following example. With regard to English, we might make a hypothesis that adjectives always precede nouns. In support of this hypothesis, we could produce the following acceptable uses:

a good man

a dead tree

But against our hypothesis, we would find the following acceptable sentences:

The man is good.

The tree is dead.

where our adjectives do not precede the nouns they modify. In addition, a careful study of the language would produce further samples such as:

life everlasting

mission impossible

where, once again, the position of the adjective contradicts our original hypothesis. When we have carried out a detailed examination of adjectives in English, we are in a position to say that adjectives in English are used in two main ways: (a) they can be used attributively, that is before a noun, as in:

a good man

and: (*b*) they can be used predicatively, that is following a verb, as in:

The man is good.

Such rules would cover the uses of most adjectives in English. It would be necessary, however, to add a further rule. In English a finite number of adjectives, borrowed from other languages or used in fixed phrases, follow the nouns they modify. Such a finite list would include:

astronomer royal

attorney general

court martial

heir apparent

prince imperial

princess royal

What is language?

Put at its simplest, a language is a set of signals by which we communicate. Human beings are not the only species to have an elaborate communication system. Bees communicate about honey and about the siting of a new hive; chimpanzees can use vocalisations to warn of danger, to signal the finding of food or to indicate attitudes to mating; and dolphins can communicate information on food and danger by means of whistles and clicks. It is not possible in a short book to illustrate all the similarities and differences between human and animal communication. Nor would it prove fruitful to discuss whether human languages developed from earlier, simpler signalling systems. The evidence is just not available. Language seems to be as old as our species. It is not so much that we have missing links in a chain from simple communication system to complex human language. It is the chain that is missing and all we have are a few intriguing links. What we can say with confidence is that even if human languages do not differ in *essence* from animal communication, they certainly differ in *degree*. Nothing in the animal kingdom even approximates to human language for flexibility, complexity, precision, productivity and sheer quantity. Humans have learnt to make infinite use of finite means.

There are a number of other general points that are worth making about language. First, human language is not only a vocal system of communication. It can be expressed in writing, with the result that it is not limited in time or space. Secondly, each language is both arbitrary and systematic. By this we mean that no two languages behave in exactly the same way yet each language has its own set of rules. Again, a number of examples will clarify this point. The word for 'water' is 'eau' in French, 'uisce' in Gaelic. There is no intrinsic relationship between any of these words and the chemical compound H_2O which we know as water. The choice of word is arbitrary, that is non-predictable, but speakers of French and Gaelic regularly and habitually use the word from their language to refer to H_2O. The same is true with regard to sentences. In English, we say:

I am hungry.

in French:

J'ai faim. (literally, I have hunger)

and in Gaelic:

Tá ocras orm. (literally, Be hunger on me)

There is no way in which we could say that one is more 'natural' or more 'appropriate' than either of the others. Languages are arbitrary in their selection and combination of items but systematic in that similar ideas are expressed in similar ways, thus:

English: I am thirsty.
French: J'ai soif. (literally, I have thirst)
Gaelic: Tá tart orm. (literally, Be thirst on me)

And finally, there are no primitive or inferior languages. People may live in the most primitive conditions but all languages appear to be equally complex and all are absolutely adequate to the needs of their users. It used to be believed that somewhere in the world would be found a simple language, a sort of linguistic missing link between animal communication and the language of technologically advanced societies. People have been found in remote parts of Papua New Guinea and in the Amazon Basin whose way of life has not changed for thousands of years and yet their languages are as subtle, as highly organised, as flexible and as useful as those found in any other part of the world.

Language and medium

A language is an abstraction based on the linguistic behaviour of its users. It is not to be equated precisely with speech because no speaker has total mastery of the entire system and every speaker is capable of using the language inadequately through tiredness, illness or inattention. All normal children of all races learn to speak the language of their community, so speech has often been seen as the primary medium of language. The abstract system which is language can also be realised as writing, and although speech and writing have much in common, they are not to be equated or hierarchically ordered. Many books will claim that speech is 'primary' and this is true in a number of ways:

(a) writing is a relatively recent development in human societies
(b) thousands of speech communities rely solely on speech
(c) all of us speak a great deal more than we write
(d) although we acquire speech without conscious effort, learning to read and write is usually less spontaneous and less automatic

It is not, however, 'primary' if we interpret 'primary' to mean 'more important'. Speech and writing are not in competition. They are complementary and both are necessary in a technologically advanced society. We can sum up the relationship between language and its mediums in a diagram as shown in Fig. 1:

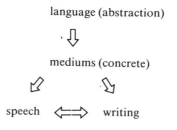

language (abstraction)

mediums (concrete)

speech <===> writing

FIG. 1: The relationship between language and its mediums

The diagram indicates that, although speech and writing are in theory distinct, they can and do influence each other. A simple example of this is that pronunciation is often affected by spelling. A word like 'often', for example, is now frequently pronounced with a 't' because of influence from the written medium.

Consider briefly the main differences between speech and writing, the two main mediums in which language is realised:

Speech	Writing
Composed of sounds	Composed of letters/signs
Makes use of intonation, pitch, rhythm, tempo	Makes use of punctuation and other graphological devices like italics
Produced effortlessly – no tools required	Produced with effort – tools required

Speech	*Writing*
Transitory	Relatively permanent
Perceived by the ear	Perceived by the eye
Addressee present	Addressee absent
Immediate feedback	Feedback delayed
Meaning helped by context, body movement, gestures	Meaning must be made clear within the context
Spontaneous	Not spontaneous
Associative	Logical

Such a list is sufficient to indicate that speech and writing are very different mediums. Furthermore, they can function independently of each other. We do not have to speak a language in order to read and write it. Nor does an ability to speak a language give a person automatic access to writing. Yet there are links between the mediums. Most writing systems are based on speech. As far as English is concerned, there is a *rough* equivalence between sounds and letters. Thus, most people can distinguish three sounds in the composition of the word that is written 'bat' and a different three in the word that is written 'pen'. The equivalence between sounds and letters is not, however, very close in English. We find, for example, only three sounds in the following words of five letters:

knead

rough

In addition, the sounds of these words can be represented in more than one way, so that 'need' is pronounced in exactly the same way as 'knead' and 'ruff' sounds exactly the same as 'rough'. Nor are these the only mismatches that occur between English sounds and letters. The 'ee' sound can be represented in at least six different ways:

beef

chief

deceive

even

machine

meat

and the 's' sound of 'sand' can be represented by both 's' and 'c':

ceiling

sealing

Most European languages are 'alphabetic', that is, there is a link between sounds and letters, but other links are possible. In Chinese the link is between a unit of meaning and a character:

下   down

上   up

人   man

言   word

'Man' and 'word', however, can be combined to make 'honest':

信

Chinese speakers from different parts of China may pronounce these characters differently but the written character always has the same meaning. A comparison with European languages may be helpful here. Although English, French and Gaelic are all alphabetic languages, they have all borrowed the numerical symbols 1,2,3 . . . from Arabic. The English write them 'one, two, three', the French 'un, deux, trois' and the Irish 'aon, dá, trí' and each group pronounces them differently. Yet all users interpret the symbols 1,2,3 . . . in the same way.

The components of language

When a parrot utters words or phrases in our language, we understand them although it is reasonably safe to assume that the parrot does not. The parrot may be able to reproduce intelligible units from the spoken medium but has no awareness of the abstract system behind the medium. Similarly, if we hear a stream of sounds in a language we do not know, we may recognise by the tone of voice whether the person is angry or annoyed but the exact meaning eludes us. To have mastery of a language, therefore, means being able to produce an infinite number of language patterns which are comprehensible to other users of the language, and in addition, being able to decipher the infinity of language patterns produced by other users of the language. It is thus a two-way process involving both production and reception.

As far as speech is concerned, the process involves associating sounds with meaning and meaning with sounds. With writing, on the other hand, language competence involves the association of a meaning (and sometimes sounds) with a sign, a visual symbol. Thus, our study of language will involve us in an appraisal of all of the following levels of language:

language
↓
phonology   – sounds
↕
morphology   – meaningful combinations of sounds
↕
lexis   – words
↕
syntax   – meaningful combinations of words
↕
semantics   – meaning

When we have examined these levels and the way they interact, we will have acquired the necessary tools to study languages in general (linguistics), the variety in language and the uses to which people put languages (sociolinguistics), the ways in which people teach and learn languages (applied linguistics) and the value of the study of language in understanding the human mind (psycholinguistics).

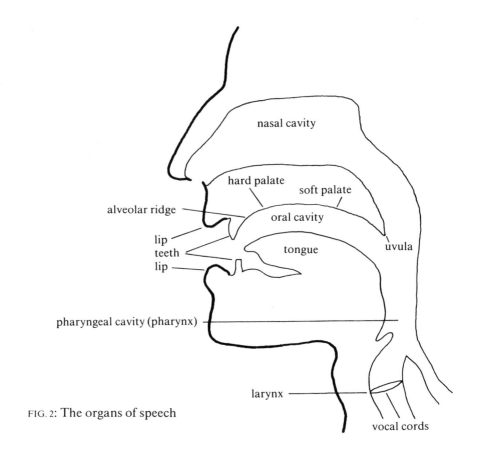

nasal cavity

hard palate

soft palate

alveolar ridge

oral cavity

lip

teeth

tongue

uvula

lip

pharyngeal cavity (pharynx)

larynx

vocal cords

FIG. 2: The organs of speech

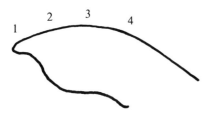

KEY:
1. Tip
2. Blade (or lamina) – lies opposite the alveolar ridge when the tongue is at rest
3. Front – lies opposite the hard palate
4. Back (or dorsum) – lies opposite the soft palate

FIG. 3: Subdivisions of the tongue

Chapter 2

Phonology

PHONOLOGY INVOLVES two studies: the study of the production, transmission and reception of speech sounds, a discipline known as 'phonetics', and the study of the sounds and sound patterns of a specific language, a discipline known as 'phonemics'. We shall examine both, the first in Chapter 2 and the second in Chapter 3.

Phonetics

Human beings are capable of producing an infinite number of sounds but no language uses more than a small proportion of this infinite set and no two human languages make use of exactly the same set of sounds. When we speak, there is continuous movement of such organs as the tongue, the velum (soft palate), the lips and the lungs. We put spaces between individual words in the written medium but there are no similar spaces in speech. Words are linked together in speech and are normally perceived by one who does not know the language (or by a machine) as an uninterrupted stream of sound. We shall, metaphorically, slow the process down as we examine the organs of speech and the types of sound that result from using different organs.

The organs of speech

Figure 2 shows the main organs of speech: the jaw, the lips, the teeth, the teeth ridge (usually called the alveolar ridge), the tongue, the hard palate, the soft palate (the velum), the uvula, the pharynx, the larynx and the vocal cords. The mobile organs are the lower jaw, the lips, the tongue, the velum, the uvula, the pharynx and the vocal cords and, although it is possible to learn to move each of these at will, we have most control over the jaw, lips and tongue. The tongue is so important in the production of speech sounds that, for ease of reference, it has been divided into four main areas, the tip, the blade (or lamina), the front and the back as shown in Fig. 3.

Sounds could not occur without air. The air required for most sounds comes from the lungs and is thus egressive ('going out'). Certain sounds in languages can, however, be made with air sucked in through the mouth. Such sounds are called ingressive ('going in'). The sound of disgust in English, a click often written 'Tch! Tch!', is made on an ingressive air stream. Coming from the lungs the air stream passes through the larynx, which is popularly referred to as the 'Adam's apple'. Inside the larynx are two folds of ligament and tissue which make up the vocal cords. These can, by muscular action, be held in five positions as illustrated in Fig. 4 below. Position 1 involves the cords being wide open as in deep breathing. Position 2 involves the cords being open, the position for voiceless (that is, breathy) sounds. Position 3 involves the cords coming together loosely and vibrating. This is the position for voiced sounds. Position 4 narrows the cords into the position used in whispering. If the cords are held tightly together (position 5) and released sharply, we produce what is known as a glottal plosive, a sound that occurs frequently in Arabic.

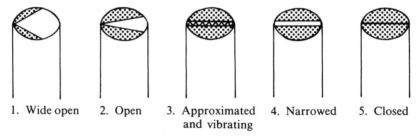

| 1. Wide open | 2. Open | 3. Approximated and vibrating | 4. Narrowed | 5. Closed |

FIG. 4: Possible positions of the vocal cords

Vowels and consonants

Sounds can be divided into two main types. A vowel is a sound that needs an open air passage in the mouth. The air passage can be modified in terms of shape with different mouth and tongue shapes producing different vowels. A consonant is formed when the air stream is restricted or stopped at some point between the vocal cords and the lips. The central sound in the word 'cat' is a vowel. The first and third sounds are consonants. More will be said about vowels and consonants in the course of this chapter but these rough definitions will serve our purpose temporarily.

Articulation

Articulatory settings

Just as each language uses a unique set of sounds from the total inventory of sounds capable of being made by humans, so too each group of speakers has a preferred pronunciation. In English, the most frequently used consonants are formed on or near the alveolar ridge; in French, the favoured consonants are made against the teeth; whereas in India many sounds are made with the tip of the tongue curling towards the hard palate, thus producing the retroflex sounds so characteristic of Indian languages. The most frequently occurring sounds in a language help to determine the position of the jaw, tongue, lips and possibly even body stance when speaking. A speaker will always sound foreign in his or her pronunciation of a language if the articulatory setting of its native speakers has not been adopted.

Manner of articulation

The ears can judge sounds very precisely, distinguishing the pure resonance of a tuning fork from the buzzing sound of a bee or the sharp report of a gun. More important for speech, perhaps, we can also distinguish between the voiceless sounds like 'p' and 't' in 'pat' and the voiced sounds like 'b' and 'd' in 'bad' or between the voiceless 'p' in 'pat' and the nasal 'm' in 'mat'. Speech exploits all these abilities and many more and scholars have devised ways of classifying sounds according to the way they are made.

The first obstacle the air meets in the vocal tract is in the glottis (the gap between the vocal cords). The vocal cords may be open, in which case the sound will be *voiceless*, or closely approximated, in which case the sound will be *voiced*. The vocal tract is a resonance chamber and different sounds can be produced by changing the shape of the chamber. If you study the various types of closure below, it will help you to describe the different types of sound you can make.

Plosives: These involve complete closure at some point in the mouth. Pressure builds up behind the closure and when the air is suddenly released a plosive is made. In English, three types of closure occur resulting in three sets of plosives. The closure can be made by the two lips, producing the bilabial plosives /p/* and /b/; it can be made by the tongue pressing against the alveolar ridge, producing

* Phonetic symbols are, by convention, indicated by placing them between two oblique strokes. An explanation of the International Phonetic Alphabet is given on pp. 19–22.

the alveolar plosives /t/ and /d/ and it can be made by the back of the tongue pressing against the soft palate, producing the velar plosives /k/ and /g/.

Fricatives: These sounds are the result of incomplete closure at some point in the mouth. The air escapes through a narrowed channel with audible friction. If you approximate the upper teeth to the lower lip and allow the air to escape you can produce the labio-dental fricatives /f/ and /v/. Again, if you approximate the tip of the tongue to the alveolar ridge, you can produce the alveolar fricatives /s/ and /z/.

Trills: These involve intermittent closure. Sounds can be produced by tapping the tongue repeatedly against a point of contact. If you roll the /r/ at the beginning of a word saying:

r.r.r.roaming

you are tapping the curled front of the tongue against the alveolar ridge producing a trill which is, for example, characteristic of some Scottish pronunciations of English.

Laterals: These sounds also involve partial closure in the mouth. The air stream is blocked by the tip of the tongue but allowed to escape around the sides of the tongue. In English, the initial /l/ sound in 'light' is a lateral; so is the final sound in 'full'.

Nasals: These sounds involve the complete closure of the mouth. The velum is lowered, diverting the air through the nose. In English, the vocal cords vibrate in the production of nasals and so English nasals are voiced. The three nasals in English are /m/ as in 'mat', /n/ as in 'no' and /ŋ/ as in 'sing'.

Affricates: Affricates are a combination of sounds. Initially there is complete closure as for a plosive. This is then followed by a slow release with friction, as for a fricative. The sound at the beginning of 'chop' is a voiceless affricate represented by the symbol /tʃ/. We make the closure as for /t/ and then release the air slowly. The sound at the beginning and end of 'judge' is a voiced affricate, represented by the symbol /dʒ/.

Frictionless continuants: In making the /r/ sound associated with BBC English, the closure is made as for the fricatives /s/ and /z/ but the air is released with less pressure. In BBC English (for a discussion of this term see below, pp. 26–32), this sound cannot occur at the end of a word.

Semi-vowels: The sounds that begin the words 'you' and 'wet' are made without closure in the mouth. To this extent, they are vowel-like. They normally occur at the beginning of a word or syllable, however, and thus behave functionally like consonants. The semi-vowels are represented by the symbols /j/ and /w/.

All sounds can be subdivided into *continuants*, that is, sounds which can be continued as long as one has breath: vowels, fricatives, laterals, trills, frictionless continuants; and *non-continuants*, that is, sounds which one cannot prolong: plosives, affricates and semi-vowels.

Place of articulation

The eight commonest places of articulation are:

Bilabial: Where the lips come together as in the sounds /p/, /b/ and /m/.

Labiodental: Where the lower lip and the upper teeth come together, as for the sounds /f/ and /v/.

Dental: Where the tip or the blade of the tongue comes in contact with the upper teeth as in the pronunciation of the initial sounds in 'thief' and 'then', represented by the symbols /θ/ and /ð/.

Alveolar: Where the tip or blade of the tongue touches the alveolar ridge which is directly behind the upper teeth. In English, the sounds made in the alveolar region predominate in the language. By this we mean that the most frequently occurring consonants /t, d, s, z, n, l, r/ are all made by approximating the tongue to the alveolar ridge.

Palato-alveolar: As the name suggests, there are two points of contact for these sounds. The tip of the tongue is close to the alveolar ridge while the front of the tongue is concave to the roof of the mouth. In English, there are four palato-alveolar sounds, the affricates /tʃ/ and /dʒ/ and the fricatives /ʃ/ and /ʒ/, the sounds that occur, respectively, at the beginning of the word 'shut' and in the middle of the word 'measure'.

Palatal: For palatal sounds, the front of the tongue approximates to the hard palate. It is possible to have palatal plosives, fricatives, laterals and nasals, but in English the only palatal is the voiced semi-vowel /j/ as in 'you'.

Velar: For velars, the back of the tongue approximates to the soft palate. As with other points of contact, several types of sound can be made here. In English there are four consonants made in the velar region, the plosives /k,g/, the nasal /ŋ/ and the voiced semi-vowel /w/ as in 'woo'.

Uvular, pharyngeal and glottal sounds occur frequently in world languages. They are not, however, significant in English and so will not be described in detail. They will, however, be illustrated in Fig. 7 which will summarise all the data presented above.

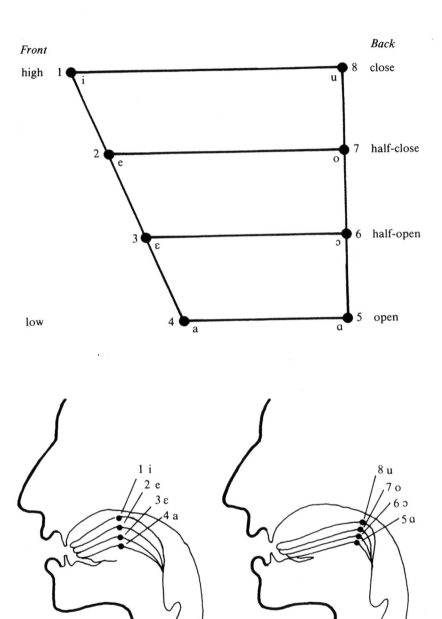

FIG. 5: Cardinal Vowel Chart – representing tongue positions

The International Phonetic Alphabet

A regular, consistent, economical system of notation is necessary for describing the sounds that occur in speech and the best-known is the International Phonetic Alphabet (IPA) chart. This alphabet is based on the ordinary roman alphabet, supplemented by other symbols so as to provide scholars with techniques for representing unambiguously all possible sounds.

Vowels cannot be classified by touch because they demand an open air passage through the mouth. They are therefore defined largely by auditory criteria. The most useful method of describing vowels is in terms of the 'Cardinal Vowel Chart'. This chart is a stylised representation of the cubic area of the mouth and it allows us to describe vowels with considerable precision. Figure 5 illustrates the eight primary cardinal vowels, with the dots indicating the highest point of the tongue during the pronunciation of each vowel. High vowels are made with the tongue close to the palate; low vowels are made with the tongue lowered from the palate, and this automatically entails the opening of the mouth. The following descriptions put into words the facts illustrated above.

Cardinal Vowel One is usually referred to as **C1** and represented by /i/. C1 is a front close vowel made with the lips spread. The vowel sound in English 'tree' is similar in quality to C1.

C2 is a front half-close vowel represented by /e/. The initial vowel in 'acorn' is similar in quality to C2.

C3 is a front half-open vowel made with spread lips. It is similar in quality to the vowel sound in English 'get' and is represented by /ɛ/.

C4 is an open front vowel represented by /a/. It is made with spread lips and is the lowest vowel capable of being made in the front of the mouth.

C5 is a low back vowel made with neutrally open lips. It is represented by /ɑ/ and is similar in quality to the vowel sound in the southern British pronunciation of 'dance'.

C6 is a half-open back vowel made with slightly rounded lips and represented by /ɔ/. It is similar in quality to the English vowel sound in 'dawn'.

C7 is a half-close back vowel made with rounded lips. It is represented by /o/.

C8 is a close back vowel made with very closely rounded lips. It is represented by /u/ and is the furthest back, closest vowel we are capable of making.

There are no near equivalents of C4, C7 and C8 in southern British English but an approximation of their quality can be given. C4 is similar in quality to the vowel in the Scottish pronunciation of 'dance'; C7 is similar in quality to a Scottish pronunciation of 'no'; C8 has not got an English analogue. It resembles the vowel sound in 'cool' but is most similar to the sound in French 'boule'.

As well as the primary cardinals, there are eight secondary cardinal vowels, as shown in Fig. 6:

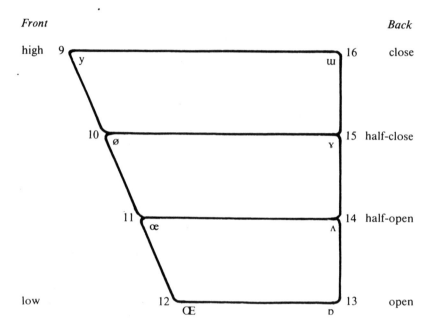

FIG. 6: Secondary cardinal vowels

These vowels are made in exactly the same positions as C1 to C8 but their lip positions are different. Thus C9 is the most advanced and the closest vowel capable of being made. It differs from C1 in that it is made with closely rounded lips. C16, on the other hand, is made in exactly the same way as C8 but the sound is made with the lips widely spread.

With these cardinal vowels as guides, any vowel from any language can be described in terms of its proximity to a cardinal vowel. To place vowels accurately demands a good ear and a fair amount of practice, but once the skill has been acquired, it is possible to show the relationship between one vowel and another with considerable precision.

It is quite a lot easier to describe and place consonants because one can feel the type of closure made in the mouth. Figure 7 (on p. 22) illustrates the main consonants that occur in languages and the symbols used to represent them. Additional symbols exist to represent more unusual sounds, such as the clicks that occur in some southern Bantu languages, but the consonant chart (Fig. 7) is adequate for the representation of the majority of sounds.

It may prove useful to offer a summary to guide the reader in the techniques to select in describing sounds. In describing a vowel it is important to state:

(1) the length of the vowel, that is, whether it is long or short
(2) whether the vowel is oral or nasal*
(3) the highest point of the tongue
(4) the degree of closeness
(5) the shape of the lips

Thus the vowel sound in 'tree' would be classified as a long, oral, front, close, unrounded vowel. The vowel in 'doom' would be a long, oral, back, close rounded vowel. It is well to remember that when the front of the tongue is raised towards the hard palate we have a *front* vowel. When the back of the tongue is raised towards the soft palate, we have a *back* vowel. If the centre of the tongue is raised towards the juncture between the hard and soft palates, then we have a central vowel. The vowel sound in the word 'the' is a central vowel and would be described as short, oral, central, half-open, with neutrally spread lips.

In describing consonants, one should state:

(1) the type of air stream used (in English *all* speech sounds are made on an egressive air stream although certain sounds of disgust and annoyance are made on an ingressive air stream)
(2) the position of the vocal cords (apart for voiceless sounds, approximated and vibrating for voiced sounds)
(3) the position of the velum (raised for oral sounds, lowered for nasal; that is, we must state whether a consonant is oral or nasal)
(4) the manner of articulation (for example plosive, fricative, and so on)
(5) the place of articulation (for example bilabial, alveolar, and so on)

Thus, if we were asked to describe the initial sound in 'buy' and the final sound in 'tin' we would say that /b/ is made on an egressive air stream and is voiced, oral, plosive and bilabial, and that /n/ is also uttered on an egressive air stream and is voiced, nasal and alveolar.

---

* All English vowels are oral.

	Bi-labial	Labio-dental	Dental and alveolar	Retroflex	Palato-alveolar	Alveolo-palatal	Palatal	Velar	Uvular	Pharyngeal	Glottal
Plosive	p b		t d	ʈ ɖ			c ɟ	k g	q G		ʔ
Nasal	m	ɱ	n	ɳ			ɲ	ŋ	N		
Lateral fricative			ɬ ɮ								
Lateral non-fricative			l	ɭ			ʎ				
Rolled			r						R		
Flapped			ɾ	ɽ					R		
Fricative	ɸ β	f v	θ ð s z ɹ	ʂ ʐ	ʃ ʒ	ɕ ʑ	ç j	x ɣ	χ ʁ	ħ ʕ	h ɦ
Frictionless continuants and semi-vowels	w ɥ	ʋ	ɹ				j (ɥ)	(w)	ʁ		

FIG. 7: The IPA Chart

Suprasegmentals

As well as the sounds that occur in speech, a number of other phenomena are of interest to the linguist. The most significant of these, pitch, stress, tone, intonation and tempo, are called 'suprasegmental features' because they accompany speech sounds and are sometimes a feature of the entire utterance rather than of any individual sound.

Pitch refers to the normal melodic height of an individual's speech. In English, higher than usual pitch for a speaker is usually associated with excitement or strain.

Human speech may be considered as a succession of syllables, some of which are more strongly stressed than others. Thus, in the word 'debatable', it is the second of the four syllables that receives most emphasis. World languages seem to be divided into two types, 'syllable-timed' languages like French where syllables are produced at regular intervals of time and where stresses occur randomly; and 'stress-timed' languages like English where stresses occur at regular intervals with a random number of syllables occurring between stresses. These differences can be illustrated by looking at the regular number of syllables in the following French couplet:

```
1   2    3    4 5   6 7   8    9   10 11 12
Sur son dos, ou livrant à leurs fiers appétits
1   2 3  4    5    6    7 8   9 10  11   12
Le trésor toujours prêt des mamelles pendantes.
```
Charles Baudelaire (1821–67)

Each line has twelve syllables. In the following English couplet, written at approximately the same time, we find four main stresses in each line:

Lóve is enoúgh: though the Wórld be a-wáning, (11 syllables)

And the wóods have no vóice but the voíce of compláining (13)
William Morris (1834–96)

but, even in two consecutive lines, the number of syllables varies from eleven to thirteen.

In so-called 'tone-languages', relative pitch can distinguish meanings. In many of the Bantu languages, for example, the word for 'house' differs from the word for 'thread' in terms of pitch difference only. Tone languages make systematic use of high, low, rising and falling pitch to distinguish meanings. Pitch is not systematically employed in this way in English although, on occasion, different meanings can be carried by changes of pitch or stress as in the sentence:

I don't like him because of his money.

If we use a rising pitch and extra stress on 'because', the sentence means that I like him but my liking is not related to the fact that he has money. If we do not stress 'because' the sentence means that I do not like him and his money is responsible for my dislike.

Intonation is associated with pitch in that it involves speech melody over an utterance. The usual intonation for a statement in English involves a slow fall:

I don't like him.

In questions, however, a rise in pitch is involved:

Do you like him?

The tempo or speed of an utterance is usually associated with a speaker's frame of mind. Increased speed may suggest excitement; reduced speed may imply boredom, tiredness or a threat.

The suprasegmentals mentioned here will not be discussed further, but references are provided in the bibliography for readers interested in pursuing this subject.

Exercises

1. Give the correct technical terms for the sounds made in the following ways:
   (a) both lips coming together
   (b) the bottom lip and top teeth coming together
   (c) the tongue touching the upper teeth ridge
   (d) the tongue touching the hard palate
   (e) the tongue touching the soft palate

2. Give the correct technical term for the sounds resulting from the following closures:
   (a) complete closure followed by slow release of air
   (b) complete closure of the oral cavity with the air diverted through the nose
   (c) partial closure where the air stream is blocked by the tip of the tongue but allowed to escape round the sides of the tongue
   (d) incomplete closure
   (e) complete closure followed by a sudden release of air

3. Give the symbol for each of the following sounds and give an example of its use in an English word:

(a) voiced bilabial plosive
(b) bilabial nasal
(c) voiceless labiodental fricative
(d) alveolar lateral
(e) high front unrounded vowel
(f) high back rounded vowel
(g) voiced alveolar fricative
(h) voiced frictionless continuant
(i) voiceless velar plosive
(j) voiced dental fricative

4. Each of the following sets contains an inappropriate member. Pick it out and say why it is inappropriate.

(a) m, n, ŋ, b
(b) b, p, n, t
(c) b, m, p, s
(d) l, f, v, s, z
(e) l, o, e, ɛ
(f) i, o, ɛ, e
(g) t, d, l, n, p
(h) t, d, p, f, s
(i) b, d, z, r, s
(j) t, k, ŋ, g

5. Describe the similarities and differences in the sounds represented by the underlined elements in the following sets. (Remember you are dealing with *sounds* and not *letters*.)

(a) lea_f_   lea_v_es
(b) as_s_ure   a_z_ure
(c) sa_d_   sa_t_
(d) _s_eat   _s_et
(e) _j_ut   _sh_ut
(f) no_t_ion   no_dd_ing
(g) rou_gh_   ru_b_
(h) _f_eel   _f_all
(i) _v_ine   _w_ine
(j) si_ng_   si_n_

Chapter 3

The sounds
of English

As was stated in Chapter 2, phonology has two aspects. We have dealt
in general terms with the production, transmission and reception of
sounds and we shall now turn our attention to the sound patterns in
English. Since Standard English has no official pronunciation, we find
considerable variation throughout the world: an American does not
sound like an Australian and neither sounds like an Englishman. It
would be impossible to cover all the variations found and so the
description will be limited to the pronunciation sanctioned in Britain
and in the United States by radio and television. What will be
described, therefore, are the network norms established by the BBC
(British Broadcasting Corporation) in Britain and by the NBC
(National Broadcasting Company) and CBS (Columbia Broadcasting
System) in the United States.

The phonemes of English

All human beings are alike, yet every human being has a unique set of
fingerprints. In a similar way, all languages make use of consonants
and vowels yet no two languages have the same set of distinct sounds
or phonemes. A phoneme is not one specific sound but it is like the
common denominators of all realisations of a specific sound. Let us
take an example. If we say the words:

   pin   spin   nip

aloud, we realise that the 'p' sounds are all slightly different. The 'p' in
'pin' is pronounced with a lot of breath, the 'p' in 'spin' has qualities of
the 'b' in 'bin' and the 'p' in 'nip' is pronounced as if it were followed
by a short vowel. All these 'p' sounds are different and indeed no two
people ever pronounce 'p' in exactly the same way, but the differences
are not sufficiently great to be used to distinguish meanings in English.
We say, therefore, that all the 'p' sounds in English belong to the same
phoneme. If, on the other hand, we examine the words:

   pin   pen

we realise that although these words only differ in their vowel sounds they refer to distinct objects. Since these vowel sounds can be used to distinguish many words:

din den
kin ken
tin ten

we say that the vowels /ɪ/ and /ɛ/ are different phonemes.

The consonants of English

One method of establishing the phonemes of a language is by means of minimal pairs. An illustration will help to explain this. In English, we have the word *pan* and the word *ban*. These words differ fairly fundamentally in meaning but, as far as the sounds go, they differ only in the initial segment. The sounds /p/ and /b/ can be shown to distinguish meaning in many pairs of words:

pet bet
pill bill
post boast
punk bunk

We can, therefore, conclude that /p/ and /b/ are distinct phonemes in English. The consonants of British and American English are essentially the same and twenty-four distinct consonants can be distinguished by means of minimal pairs. A list such as:

pie buy tie die guy fie vie lie
my nigh thigh thy sigh shy rye high

allows us to isolate the following consonant phonemes: /p, b, t, d, g, f, v, l, m, n, θ, ð, s, ʃ, r, h/.

Lists such as:

chin sin win
gin tin

add /tʃ, dʒ, w/, while:

simmer sinner singer

provide us with /ŋ/ and:

rice rise

isolate /z/.

	Bilabial	Labio-dental	Dental	Alveolar	Palato-alveolar	Palatal	Velar	Glottal
Plosive	p b			t d			k g	
Nasal	m			n			ŋ	
Lateral				l				
Frictionless continuant				ɹ				
Retroflex				r				
Fricative		f v	θ ð	s z	ʃ ʒ			h
Affricate					tʃ dʒ			
Semi-vowel	w					j		

FIG. 8: The consonant phonemes of English

The remaining three phonemes are revealed by the three sets below:

leper   letter   ledger   leisure

which give us /ʒ/ and:

car   bar   far

which provide /k/, and finally:

bard   card   yard

which reveal /j/. We can summarise the above data in a table such as Fig. 8. This actually shows twenty-five symbols but both UK and US speakers use only twenty-four. The difference is in the pronunciation of 'r'. Many speakers of English use a different 'r' sound. In BBC English the sound is described as a frictionless continuant, the symbol

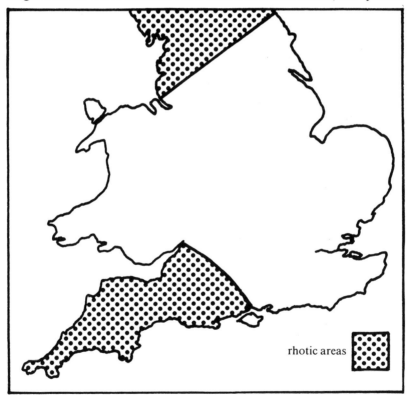

rhotic areas

FIG. 9: Approximate locations of rhotic and non-rhotic accents in England (see p. 30)

for which is /ɹ/, whereas in the US the 'r' is called 'retroflex' because the sound is made with the tip of the tongue curling towards the hard palate. There are distinct symbols for these sounds but since the sounds are not used to distinguish meaning, the same symbol /r/ can be used for both. A further point can be made about /r/. Many accents, including that favoured by the BBC, do not pronounce 'r' when it occurs at the end of a word or before a consonant. Thus the 'r' is not pronounced in 'far', 'fear', 'fir', 'for', 'fur' or in 'card', 'pert', 'shirk', 'thorn', 'hurl'. Accents which do not pronounce the 'r' in these positions are called 'non-rhotic' accents. Speakers who do pronounce the 'r' in such contexts have 'rhotic' accents. There are historical and linguistic reasons for the division of world Englishes into 'rhotic' and 'non-rhotic' but the easiest way to remember which areas of the world pronounce post-vocalic 'r' and which do not is to think of a map such as that presented in Fig. 9 (p. 29). Shaded areas to the north and/or west of the drawn lines are rhotic; areas to the south and/or east are non-rhotic. The main rhotic areas of the world are the USA, Canada, Scotland and Ireland. The main non-rhotic areas are Wales, most of England, Australia, New Zealand and Southern Africa.

The vowels of English

As might be expected, there is much greater variation in the pronunciation of vowel phonemes than is the case with consonants. The variety of British English that we have chosen to describe has twelve monophthongs and eight diphthongs whereas our US variety has ten monophthongs and five diphthongs. The systems will be described first of all, and then the differences will be accounted for. Figure 10 illustrates the positions of the twelve monophthongs in British English. (The vowels of any language can be plotted using the Cardinal Vowels as a guide.) They can be described as follows:

Vowel 1 which has the phonetic symbol /i/ is a close, long, front vowel, made with spread lips. It occurs in such words as 'eat', 'seed' and 'see'.

Vowel 2 which has the phonetic symbol /ɪ/ differs from Vowel 1 in both quality and length. It is a half-close, short, front vowel made with spread lips. It is also one of the most frequently used vowels in the English language and one that is often replaced by Vowel 1 in the speech of non-native speakers. This vowel occurs in such words as 'it', 'sit' and 'city'.

Vowel 3 which has the phonetic symbol /ɛ/ is a short, front vowel produced with spread lips. It occurs in words like 'egg' and 'get' but does not occur in word-final position in English.

Vowel 4 which is represented phonetically by /æ/ is a short, front, open vowel. It is made with the lips in a neutrally open position. It occurs in words like 'add', 'sat' and, like /ɛ/, does not occur in word-final position in English.

Vowel 5 is represented by the symbol /ɑ/. It is a long, open, back vowel made with slightly rounded lips. It occurs in words like 'art', 'farther' and 'far'. This vowel does not occur in US English.

Vowel 6 is represented by the symbol /ɒ/. This is a short, open, back vowel made in British English with slightly rounded lips and in the US with neutrally open lips. It is found in words such as 'on' and 'pod' and does not occur in word-final position. In US English words such as 'card' and 'cod' are distinguished by length of vowel and by the pronunciation of 'r' in the former rather than by any intrinsic difference in vowel quality.

Vowel 7 is represented by /ɔ/. This is a long, half-open, back vowel pronounced with lip-rounding. Again, there is more lip-rounding in the British pronunciation of /ɔ/. This sound occurs in 'all', 'sawed' and 'raw'.

Vowel 8 is represented phonetically by /ʊ/. This is a short, half-close, back vowel pronounced with lip-rounding. It does not occur in word-initial position but is found in 'put' and in 'to'.

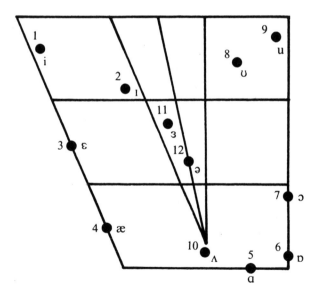

FIG. 10: The positions of the twelve monophthongs in British English

Vowel 9 is transcribed /u/. This is a long, close, back vowel produced with lip-rounding. It is found in words such as 'ooze', 'booed' and 'too'.

Vowel 10 is represented by /ʌ/. This is a short, open, centralised vowel. It does not occur in word-final position but is found in 'up' and 'bud'.

Vowel 11 does not occur in US English. It is represented by the symbol /ɜ/. It is a long, central vowel and occurs in such words as 'err', 'church' and 'sir'.

Vowel 12 is represented by /ə/ and is the only vowel sound in English with a name. /ə/ is called 'schwa'. The schwa is the most frequently occurring vowel sound in colloquial English speech, and all unstressed English vowels tend to be realised as /ə/. This is a short, central vowel which occurs in the unstressed syllables of such words as 'ago' and 'mother'.

All the vowels described above are monophthongs. This means that there is no tongue movement during the production of the vowel sound. A diphthong, however, involves the movement of the tongue from one vowel position to another. Figure 11 illustrates the diphthongs that occur in BBC English. NBC English uses only five of the eight diphthongs found in Britain.

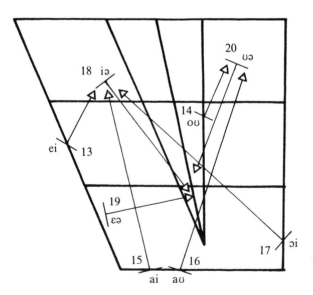

FIG. 11: Diphthongs in BBC English

Vowel	Word	UK pronunciation	US pronunciation
1	bead	bid	bid
2	bid	bɪd	bɪd
3	bed	bɛd	bɛd
4	bad	bæd	bæd
5	bard	bɑd	bɒrd
6	God	gɒd	gɒd
7	bawd	bɔd	bɔd
8	good	gʊd	gʊd
9	booed	bud	bud
10	bud	bʌd	bʌd
11	bird	bɜd	bɜrd
12	above	əbʌv	əbʌv
13	bayed	beid	beid
14	bode	boud	boud
15	bide	baid	baid
16	bowed	baʊd	baʊd
17	boy	bɔi	bɔi
18	beard	biəd	bird
19	bared	bɛəd	bɛrd
20	gourd	gʊəd	gʊrd

FIG. 12: A comparison of vowel phonemes in British and American English

Vowel 13 is represented by /ei/. Like all English diphthongs it is long. It starts close to Vowel 3 and moves towards Vowel 2. This sound occurs in such words as 'ail', 'rain' and 'day'.

Vowel 14 is represented by /ou/. It starts near the centre of the mouth in British English and moves towards Vowel 8. This diphthong is narrower and is pronounced with more lip-rounding in US English. It occurs in such words as 'oat', 'known' and 'go'.

Vowel 15 is represented by /ai/. This is a wide diphthong which starts in the region of Vowel 4 and moves towards Vowel 2. This diphthong is found in words such as 'aisle', 'fight' and 'high'.

Vowel 16 is represented by /au/. This is a wide diphthong which starts in the region of Vowel 4 and moves towards Vowel 8. It occurs in such words as 'out', 'house' and 'now'.

Vowel 17 is represented by /ɔi/. This diphthong begins in the region of Vowel 7 and moves towards Vowel 2. It occurs in such words as 'oil', 'toyed' and 'boy'.

The above are the five diphthongs shared by British and US English.

Vowel 18 is represented by /ɪə/. It is a centring vowel in that it starts near Vowel 2 and moves towards Vowel 12. This diphthong is found in such words as 'ear', 'pierce' and 'beer'. You will notice that this diphthong occurs in words which involve post-vocalic 'r'. The sound in such words would be represented by /ir/ in US English.

Vowel 19 is represented by /ɛə/. It is a centring diphthong which starts near Vowel 3 and moves towards Vowel 12. It is found in such words as 'air', 'paired' and 'there'. This sound is usually represented in US English by /ɛr/, that is, by the combination of a vowel similar in quality to Vowel 3 followed by the consonant /r/.

Vowel 20 is represented by /ʊə/ (/ʊr/ in the US). It is a centring vowel starting near Vowel 8 and moving towards Vowel 12. This diphthong does not occur in word-initial position but is found in words like 'tour' and 'moor'. With many speakers this diphthong is replaced by the monophthong /ɔ/ so that it is not uncommon to have speakers who pronounce 'Shaw', 'shore' and 'sure' in exactly the same way, as /ʃɔ/.

Until relatively recently in Britain, there was a twenty-first vowel sound, the diphthong /ɔə/. This occurred in words such as 'door' and 'floor'. Nowadays, in Britain, such words are pronounced with the monophthong /ɔ/.

These vowel data, illustrating the UK and US usages, can be summarised in tabular form. This is done in Fig. 12 (p. 33).

Consonant clusters

The English language permits a number of consonant clusters such as /dr/ and /spl/. There are restrictions on the type of combination which can occur. These can be summarised in two groups: consonant clusters in initial position, and consonant clusters in final position.

Consonant clusters in initial position

The maximum cluster of consonants (C) in an initial position in English is three, and they must be followed by a vowel (V), thus: CCCV. If there are three consonants, however, the first must be /s/, the second must come from the set /p,t,k/, and the third must come from the set /l,r,w,j/, but these can only occur in certain patterns, as shown below:

$$
s + \begin{cases} p + l \ or \ r \ or \ j \ \text{(in British English)} \\ t + r \ or \ j \ \text{(in British English)} \\ k + l \ or \ r \ or \ w \ or \ j \ \text{(in British English)}. \end{cases}
$$

The above possibilities are illustrated by the following words:

splash, sprain, spurious /spjʊərɪəs/
strain, stew /stju/
screech, sclerosis, squander /skwɒndə/ and skew /skju/

If there are only two consonants in the cluster, the first must come from the set /p, t, k, b, d, g, f, v, θ, s, ʃ, h/ in the following patterns. The normal orthography is used but the reader is reminded that sounds and not spellings are referred to:

p + l/r/j	*as in*	play, pray, pure
t + r/j/w	*as in*	tray, tune, twin
k + l/r/j/w	*as in*	climb, crab, cure, queen
b + l/r/j	*as in*	blue, bruise, beauty
g + l/r/j/w	*as in*	glow, grow, argue, Gwen
f + l/r/j	*as in*	fly, fry, fury
v + j	*as in*	view
θ + r/j/w	*as in*	through, thews, thwart
s + l/j/w/p/t/k/m/n	*as in*	slow, suit, sweet, spoil, steal, sky smother, snow
ʃ + r	*as in*	shred
h + j	*as in*	huge

Consonant clusters in final position

English permits up to four consonants in word final position, so we have CCCVCCCC as a possible English word. Such words are uncommon but 'strengths' illustrates the pattern. The following types of clusters can be established, starting with VCC:

p + t/θ/s	*as in*	swept, depth, caps
t + θ/s	*as in*	eighth, puts
k + t/s	*as in*	packed, box
b + d/z	*as in*	rubbed, nibs /nɪbz/
d + z/θ	*as in*	feeds, breadth
g + d/z	*as in*	sagged, rugs
tʃ + t	*as in*	itched /ɪtʃt/
m + p/d/f/θ/z	*as in*	limp, drummed, nymph, warmth, rims
n + t/d/tʃ/dʒ/θ/s/z	*as in*	mint, lined, lunch, hinge, tenth, mince, buns

ŋ + k/d/z/θ	*as in*	mink, longed, bangs, length
l + p/t/k/b/d/tʃ/dʒ/ m/n/f/v/θ/s/z/ʃ	*as in*	help, guilt, bulk, bulb, build, filch, bulge, helm, sullen, elf, shelve, health, else, heels, Welsh
f + t/θ/s	*as in*	left, fifth, oafs
v + d/z	*as in*	loved, gives
θ + t/s	*as in*	earthed, hearths
ð + d/z	*as in*	bathed /beiðd/, oaths
s + p/t/k	*as in*	wasp, waste, rusk
z + d	*as in*	seized
ʃ + t	*as in*	wished
ʒ + d	*as in*	rouged /ruʒd/

The VCCC pattern is quite frequent in English although it is not found as widely in the language as the VCC pattern. It is not necessary to go into the same detail for VCCC as for VCC but it can be claimed that the following list comprehends all forty-nine possibilities:

pts	*as in*	scripts	/skrɪpts/
pst	*as in*	lapsed	/læpst/
pθs	*as in*	depths	/dɛpθs/
tst	*as in*	blitzed	/blɪtst/
tθs	*as in*	widths	/wɪtθs/
dst	*as in*	midst	/mɪdst/
kts	*as in*	facts	/fækts/
kst	*as in*	next	/nɛkst/
ksθ	*as in*	sixth	/sɪksθ/
mpt	*as in*	bumped	/bʌmpt/
mps	*as in*	limps	/lɪmps/
mfs	*as in*	nymphs	/nɪmfs/
ntθ	*as in*	thousandth	/θaʊsəntθ/
nts	*as in*	pints	/paɪnts/
ndz	*as in*	finds	/faɪndz/
ntʃt	*as in*	lunched	/lʌntʃt/
ndʒd	*as in*	lunged	/lʌndʒd/
nθs	*as in*	tenths	/tɛnθs/
nst	*as in*	minced	/mɪnst/
nzd	*as in*	cleansed	/klɛnzd/
ŋst	*as in*	amongst	/əmʌŋst/

ŋkt	*as in*	linked	/lɪŋkt/
ŋkθ	*as in*	length	/lɛŋkθ/
ŋks	*as in*	thanks	/θæŋks/
lpt	*as in*	helped	/hɛlpt/
lps	*as in*	gulps	/gʌlps/
lts	*as in*	wilts	/wɪlts/
lkt	*as in*	milked	/mɪlkt/
lks	*as in*	silks	/sɪlks/
lbz	*as in*	bulbs	/bʌlbz/
ldz	*as in*	welds	/wɛldz/
ltʃt	*as in*	filched	/fɪltʃt/
ldʒd	*as in*	bulged	/bʌldʒd/
lmd	*as in*	overwhelmed	/ouvəwɛlmd/
lmz	*as in*	helms	/hɛlmz/
lnz	*as in*	gallons	/gælnz/
lfs	*as in*	sylphs	/sɪlfs/
lfθ	*as in*	twelfth	/twɛlfθ/
lvd	*as in*	shelved	/ʃɛlvd/
lvz	*as in*	elves	/ɛlvz/
lθs	*as in*	health's	/hɛlθs/
lst	*as in*	waltzed	/wɔlst/
fts	*as in*	lifts	/lɪfts/
fθs	*as in*	fifths	/fɪfθs/
spt	*as in*	gasped	/gaspt/
sps	*as in*	lisps	/lɪsps/
sts	*as in*	lasts	/lɑsts/
skt	*as in*	asked	/ɑskt/
sks	*as in*	risks	/rɪsks/

The VCCCC pattern, where four consonants occur at the end of a word or syllable is rare in English and is only found when the inflectional endings /s/ and /t/ are added to a VCCC form as in 'thousandths' /θauzəntθs/, exempts /ɛksɛmpts/ or glimpsed /glɪmpst/.

Stress

Information has already been provided on pitch, stress, intonation, and tempo (see pp. 23–4) so here we shall simply emphasise the fact that in English a shift in stress pattern can indicate a shift in the way a word functions. Thus, when 'permit' functions as a noun, the stress is on the first syllable:

This is your 'permit.

When it is used as a verb, however, the word takes the stress on the second syllable:

Per'mit me to say.

Other words which use a similar stress change to indicate a change of function are:

Noun	Verb
'accent	ac'cent
'contract	con'tract
'export	ex'port
'import	im'port
'object	ob'ject
'subject	sub'ject

Adjectives are also sometimes distinguished from verbs by a difference in stress:

Adjective	Verb
'absent	ab'sent
con'summate	consum'mate
'perfect	per'fect
'present	pre'sent

Summary

In this chapter, methods of describing the sound system of English have been examined. Each model of grammar has its own preferences and so different descriptions will emphasise different aspects of phonology. The account given above, however, is compatible with all models of grammar for English and will be extended in subsequent chapters where some of the most influential descriptions of English produced in the last fifty years are examined.

Exercises

---

1. Supply pairs of English words which can be distinguished by the following sets of consonants. (For example, a minimal pair for /p/ and /b/ could be 'pear' and 'bear'. Remember that you are dealing

with *sounds* and not *spellings*, so 'post' and 'boast' would also be a minimal pair.)

(1) /p/ and /b/
(2) /t/ and /d/
(3) /k/ and /g/
(4) /s/ and /z/
(5) /ʃ/ and /tʃ/
(6) /n/ and /ŋ/
(7) /m/ and /p/
(8) /n/ and /d/
(9) /r/ and /l/
(10) /tʃ/ and /dʒ/

2. Transcribe the following words phonemically, using BBC pronunciation.

(1) ghost
(2) among
(3) infiltrate
(4) farmyard
(5) chutney
(6) judging
(7) splendid
(8) underpinned
(9) thousandths
(10) beautiful

3. What English words are represented by the following transcriptions? Where the phonemic notation could represent more than one word, indicate the alternatives.

(1) /ʃɔt/
(2) /treʒə/
(3) /kjut/
(4) /ju/
(5) /mit/
(6) /tʃɜtʃ/
(7) /tʌŋ/
(8) /wɛðə/
(9) /dʒæz/
(10) /ɛvrɪθɪŋ/

4. Transcribe the following words in phonemic notation indicating (*a*) UK and (*b*) US pronunciation.

(1) bird
(2) grass

(3) new
(4) castle
(5) farmyard
(6) bread
(7) fair
(8) steward
(9) hall
(10) whole

5. Indicate where the main stress occurs in the following words by placing a stress mark ' before the stressed syllable. If more than one stress pattern is possible, provide the alternatives.

(1) apple
(2) division
(3) duly
(4) fashionable
(5) infiltration
(6) lobotomy
(7) photographic
(8) object
(9) university
(10) zoology

Chapter 4

Morphology

PHONOLOGY HAS BEEN DESCRIBED as the study of speech sounds and their patterns. It is a study based on the 'phoneme' or smallest significant unit of speech. Morphology is the study of morphemes, which are the smallest significant units of grammar. This definition becomes more comprehensible if you look at some examples. If you examine such patterns as:

(a) cat	cats
mat	mats
bat	bats

or:

(b) cook	cooked
look	looked
book	booked

you will see that in (a) plurality is indicated by adding +s to the singular noun thus:

Singular	*Plural*
cat	cat+s
mat	mat+s
bat	bat+s

In each example, there are two morphemes, the morpheme 'cat' (or the morpheme 'mat' or 'bat') and the morpheme 's' which in many English words marks the difference between singular and plural. In (b) there is the following pattern:

Present	*Past*
cook	cook+ed
look	look+ed
book	book+ed

where the 'ed' morpheme indicates the past tense for many English verbs.

Free and bound morphemes

If you look at a number of other examples you can establish different categories of morpheme. The words:

unmanly

meaningless

can be split up into:

un+man+ly

and:

mean+ing+less

In both these examples, the words are composed of three morphemes, only one of which can occur in isolation:

That *man* is very tired.

What do you *mean*?

Morphemes which can occur freely on their own are called 'free' morphemes. Morphemes which can only occur as affixes are described as 'bound' morphemes. Bound morphemes (or affixes) are divided into two types: those like 'dis-' and 'un-' which precede words (that is, free morphemes) and which are called prefixes and those like '-ly' and '-ness' which follow free morphemes and which are called suffixes.

Allomorphs

Often, morphemes which fulfil the same function have slightly different forms. If you look at the following three words:

slammed

slipped

stilted

you will notice that, in the written form, they all have the '-ed' morpheme indicating the past tense. When you pronounce these words, however, you become aware that the '-ed' morpheme has three different forms:

/slæmd/

/slɪpt/

/stɪltɪd/

/d/ in 'slammed', /t/ in 'slipped' and /ɪd/ in 'stilted'. When a morpheme has alternative forms the various forms are known as 'allomorphs'.

Take another example. Some English adjectives form their opposites by prefixing the bound morpheme 'in-':

capable	incapable
tolerant	intolerant

Often, however, the negative morpheme changes 'n' to the consonant of the word it prefixes:

legal	illegal
mobile	immobile
regular	irregular

'il-', 'im-' 'in-' and 'ir-' can thus be called allomorphs.

Derivational morphology

Morphology fulfils two main functions in English. Morphemes can be used to form new words:

beauty + ful > beautiful

danger + ous > dangerous

or to inflect verbs and nouns:

look, look+s, look+ing, look+ed

tree, tree+s

The first category is known as derivational morphology and it involves prefixation:

re + turn > return

un + true > untrue

suffixation:

man + ly > manly

wicked + ness > wickedness

or affixation involving both prefixation and suffixation:

un + speak + able > unspeakable

sub + conscious + ly > subconsciously

Commonly occurring prefixes are 'be-', 'de-', 'en-', 'ex-', 'hyper-', 'pre-', 'pro-', 're-', 'sub-', 'super-' and 'trans-'. Prefixes alter meaning but do not always change the function of the word to which they are prefixed:

Prefix	Free morpheme (Class)	Result (Class)
be	witch (n.)	bewitch (v.)
de	limit (v.)	delimit (v.)
en	rich (adj.)	enrich (v.)
ex	terminate (v.)	exterminate (v.)
hyper	market (n.)	hypermarket (n.)

Commonly occurring suffixes always change the class of the word to which they are attached:

beauty (n.) + ful	beautiful (adj.)
determine (v.) + ation	determination (n.)

Words ending in the morphemes '-acy', '-ation', '-er/-or', '-ess', '-ity', '-ment', '-ness' and '-ship' tend to be nouns:

democracy	actor	bewilderment
adoration	mistress	weakness
painter	solemnity	horsemanship

Words ending in '-ise/ize' tend to be verbs:

epitomise
hospitalise

Words ending in '-able', '-ed', '-ful', '-ical', '-ive', '-less', '-like', '-ous' and '-y' tend to be adjectives:

an enjoyable film
a polished performance
a comical episode
a diminutive person
a helpless individual
a workmanlike effort
an industrious group
a pretty girl

And words which end in '-ly' tend to be adverbs:

He ran home *quickly*.
She locked the doors *securely*.

Although the above suffixes tend to be associated with particular word classes, it is always worth remembering that, in English, it is only safe to judge the class of an item when it has been seen in context. Thus, although 'lovely' and 'friendly' end in '-ly' they function as adjectives and not as adverbs:

a lovely girl   a friendly welcome

Inflectional morphology

Whereas derivational affixes often involve a change of class – such as the verb 'attract' becoming the adjective 'attractive' – inflectional suffixes never involve a change of class. Inflectional morphology occurs with nouns, pronouns* and verbs. In nouns, inflection marks plurality in regular nouns:

book	books
chair	chairs

and the possessive of all nouns:

John	John's book/books
the man	the man's book/books
the men	the men's book/books
the builders	the builders' material/materials

Irregular nouns often form their plurals by a vowel change:

foot	feet
man	men
mouse /maʊs/	mice /maɪs/

but they form the possessive in exactly the same way as regular nouns:

the dog	the dog's tail
the mouse	the mouse's nose

There is no difference in sound between a regular noun's plural form and its possessive:

the doctor
the doctor's patients
the doctors
the doctors' patients

*Pronouns change according to such categories as plurality and case. They will be dealt with in Chapter 5.

In the written medium, however, the apostrophe indicates whether or not we are dealing with a possessive and whether or not the possessive is singular or plural.

With regard to verbs in English, inflectional suffixes are used to indicate present tense agreement:

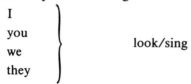

I
you
we   look/sing
they

but:

he/she/it   look+s/sing+s

and the present participle:

look+ing/sing+ing

For regular verbs the past tense and the past participle are formed by the suffix '-ed':

I look+ed/I have look+ed

whereas, with irregular verbs, the past tense and the past participle are often signalled by a vowel change or a vowel change plus a suffix:

sing	sang	sung
take	took	taken
write	wrote	written

Summary

The information on morphology can be summarised as follows:

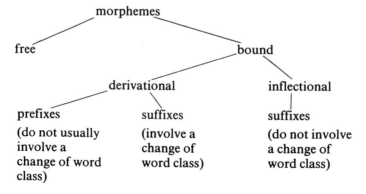

morphemes

free   bound

derivational   inflectional

prefixes   suffixes   suffixes
(do not usually   (involve a   (do not involve
involve a   change of   a change of
change of word   word class)   word class)
class)

Exercises

1. Identify the morphemes in the following words, indicating where a spelling change may be necessary when one breaks the word down into its constituents.

   (1) equalisers
   (2) inclination
   (3) befriending
   (4) transportation
   (5) endearment
   (6) predetermination
   (7) dangerously
   (8) unbelievable
   (9) protection
   (10) dehumanise

2. Pick out the bound morphemes in the following words and say whether they are derivational morphemes (D) or inflectional morphemes (I).

   (1) inflectional
   (2) terrifying
   (3) hospitalised
   (4) regularises
   (5) reviewers
   (6) respectably
   (7) represents
   (8) stifles
   (9) previewed
   (10) submariners

3. What are the main allomorphs of each of the following morphemes? Provide examples to illustrate each of the allomorphs.

   (1) -s (as in the verb 'looks')
   (2) -ed (as in the verb 'looked')
   (3) in- (as in words where the morpheme means 'not', for example 'in + eligible')

4. Segment the following words into free and bound morphemes. Say in each case whether the bound morpheme changes the word class of the free morpheme.

   (1) unbearable
   (2) moralised
   (3) tranquilisers
   (4) imprudently
   (5) width

5. Identify the inflectional (I) and derivational (D) affixes in the following words and assess their productivity (that is, say whether they can be used in the modification of many, some or few morphemes in English).

(1) non-event
(2) Assamese
(3) examination
(4) happenings
(5) multivitamin
(6) interdenominational
(7) delighted
(8) John's
(9) midsummer
(10) featureless

Chapter 5

Lexicology

LEXICOLOGY IS THE STUDY OF WORDS and, whereas many readers will be new to the study of sounds or word segments, most of us feel that we are very familiar with words. Indeed, when we think of language we tend to think about words. We often ask: 'What's the word for a stamp-collector?' or say: 'I just can't think of the right word.' As we have already seen, words are only one of the strands in language, a strand that has, in the past, been given too much attention and a strand that, because of our familiarity with it, we have often failed to study as rigorously and as objectively as other aspects of language. In this chapter, we shall try, first of all, to say what a word is. We shall then consider word-formation and word classes. Other questions relating to words – their meaning and organisation – will be dealt with in Chapter 7 when we discuss semantics.

What do we mean by 'word'?

In spite of our familiarity with 'words', it is not always easy to say what a word is. Certain scholars have suggested that a word can occur in isolation. This claim has some validity, but would 'a' or 'my' or 'if' normally occur in isolation? They would not and yet we would like to think of such items as words. Others have suggested that a word contains one unit of meaning. This is perhaps true if we think of words like 'car' or 'snow', but when we think of sets of words like 'cow', 'bull' and 'calf' or 'ewe', 'ram' and 'lamb', we become aware that the first set might be regarded as follows:

cow ⇒ + noun	bull ⇒ + noun	calf ⇒ + noun
+ bovine	+ bovine	+ bovine
+ female	+ male	+ unmarked sex

and we could establish similar patterns for the second set. It would be hard to say, looking at our patterns, that the word 'cow' contains only one unit of meaning.

A better approach to defining words is to acknowledge that there is no one totally satisfactory definition, but that we can isolate four of the most frequently implied meanings of 'word': the *orthographic* word, the *morphological* word, the *lexical* word and the *semantic* word.

(1) An *orthographic* word is one which has a space on either side of it. Thus, in the previous sentence, we have fourteen orthographic words. This definition applies only to the written medium, however, because in normal speech we rarely pause between words. Nevertheless, even in speech it is possible to isolate words by pausing between them.

(2) A *morphological* word is a unique form. It considers form only and not meaning. 'Ball', for example, is one morphological word, even though it can refer to both a bouncing object and a dance. 'Ball' and 'balls' would be two morphological words because they are not identical in form.

(3) A *lexical* word comprehends the various forms of items which are closely related by meaning. Thus, 'chair' and 'chairs' are two morphological words, but one lexical word. Similarly, 'take', 'takes', 'taking', 'taken' and 'took' are five morphological words but only one lexical word. Often in linguistics, when capital letters are used for a word, for example TAKE, it implies that we are dealing with a lexical word and so TAKE comprehends all the various forms, that is, 'take', 'takes', 'taking', 'taken' and 'took'.

(4) A *semantic* word involves distinguishing between items which may be morphologically identical but differ in meaning. We have seen above that 'ball' can have two distinct meanings. This phenomenon of 'polysemy' is common in English. Thus, 'table' can refer to a piece of furniture or to a diagram. The diagram and the piece of furniture are the same morphological word but they are two semantic words because they are not closely related in meaning.

Word-formation

We have already looked at some of the methods of word-formation in English. These can be summarised as follows:

Suffixation:	man + ly	>	manly
Prefixation:	un + true	>	untrue
Affixation:	dis + taste + ful	>	distasteful

As well as the above techniques of derivation, the commonest type of word-formation in English is called 'compounding', that is, joining two words together to form a third. Compounding frequently involves two nouns:

book + case	>	bookcase
sea + man	>	seaman
wall + paper	>	wallpaper

Occasionally, the possessive form of the first noun is used although apostrophes are not found in the compound:

bull's + eye	>	bullseye
lamb's + wool	>	lambswool

Other parts of speech can, of course, combine to form new words and we provide selective examples of these below:

noun + verb

hair + do	>	hairdo
blood + shed	>	bloodshed

adjective + noun

blue + bell	>	bluebell
hot + house	>	hothouse

adjective + verb

easy + going	>	easygoing
wide + spread	>	widespread

verb + noun

lock + jaw	>	lockjaw
scare + crow	>	scarecrow

verb + adverb

come + back	>	comeback
take + away	>	takeaway

adverb + verb

down + fall	>	downfall
out + cry	>	outcry

Often, when the compound is new, whether it involves a prefix and a word or two words, a hyphen is used between the parts:

come-back

dis-inter

but, as the compound becomes more familiar, the hyphen is dropped. The main exception to this rule is that the hyphen is often retained when two vowels come together:

co-operation

multi-ethnic

take-off

New words are formed in English by four other processes: coinages, backformations, blends and acronyms. Words can be coined from existing material to represent a new invention or development:

wireless

television

hypermarket

Often, when the coinages refer to trade-names, untraditional spellings are used:

kleenex (tissues)

sqezy (washing-up liquid)

Backformations involve the use of analogy to create forms that are similar to ones already in existence in the language. Thus, recently we have derived:

gatecrash   *from* gatecrasher

globetrot   *from* globetrotter

pop   *from* popular

Blends involve joining two words together by taking parts of both words and welding the parts into a new whole:

breakfast + lunch > brunch

chuckle   + snort > chortle

motor   + hotel > motel

The fourth technique involves creating words out of the initial letters of well-known organisations:

UNESCO   *from* United Nations Educational Scientific
          and Cultural Organisation

Laser   *from* Light Amplification by Stimulated Emission
          of Radiation

Word classes

We have looked at the *form* of some English words and we shall now sort these words into classes according to the way they *function*. One crucial generalisation has to be made first, however. Words in English can function in many different ways. Thus 'round' can be a noun in:

He won the first round.

an adjective in:

She bought a round table for the dining room.

a verb in:

They rounded the corner at eighty miles an hour.

an adverb in:

The doctor will come round this evening.

and a preposition in:

He went round the track in four minutes.

In English, it is always essential to see how a word functions in a particular example before assigning it to a word class.

In spite of the flexibility of English words, we can use test frames to distinguish a number of word classes which we shall list and then describe:

nouns

determiners

pronouns

adjectives

verbs

adverbs

prepositions

conjunctions

exclamations/interjections

A **noun** has often been defined as the name of a person, animal, place, concept or thing. Thus *Michael, tiger, Leeds, grace* and *grass* are nouns. If you wish to test an item to see if it is a noun, you can use such test frames as:

(The) . . . . . seemed nice.

(This/these) . . . . . is/are good.

little . . . . .

lovely . . . . .

ancient . . . . .

A **determiner** is an adjective-like word which precedes both adjectives and nouns and can fit into such frames as the following:

Have you . . . . . wool?

I don't want . . . . . cheese.

. . . . . cat sat on . . . . . woollen gloves.

There are five main kinds of determiners: articles such as *a/an* and *the*; demonstratives *this, that, these, those*; possessives *my, your, his, her, its, our, their*; numbers when they precede nouns as in '*one* girl', '*first* degree', '*seven* hills'; indefinite determiners such as *some, any, all, enough, no, both, each, every, few, much, more, most, fewer, less, either, neither*.

Determiners always indicate that a noun follows. Many indefinite determiners can function as other parts of speech. The words in italics below are used as determiners in column A and as pronouns in column B:

A	B
I ate *some* bread.	Give me *some*.
I haven't *any* money.	I don't want *any*.
Both parents were late.	I saw *both*.

A **pronoun** is, as its name suggests, similar to a noun in that it can take the place of a noun or a noun phrase:

John met his future wife on a train.

He met *her* on *it/one*.

Pronouns can fit into such test frames as:

. . . . . don't know your name.

Give . . . . . to . . . . . .

but the simplest test for a pronoun is to check if it can replace a noun or a noun phrase.

Pronouns in English can reflect number, case and person:

Person	Singular		Plural	
	Nominative	Accusative	Nominative	Accusative
First	I	me	we	us
Second	you	you	you	you
Third	he she it	him her it	they	them

As well as reflecting nominative and accusative cases with all personal pronouns except *you* and *it*, English also has a set of seven possessive pronouns:

Person	Singular	Plural
First	mine	ours
Second	yours	yours

	his	
Third	hers	theirs
	its	

As is clear from the two tables, natural gender is marked in the third person singular:

He lost his wallet. (that is, the man)

She lost her purse. (that is, the woman)

It lost its railway link. (that is, the city)

English has six other types of pronoun: reflexives such as *myself, themselves*; demonstratives *this, that, these, those*; interrogatives *what?, which?, who?, whom?, whose?*; relatives *that, which, who, whom, whose*; distributive pronouns which are often followed by 'of you': *all* (of you), *both* (of you), *each* (of you), *either* (of you), *neither* (of you); and a set of indefinite pronouns such as *some, any* and occasionally *so* and *such* in sentences like:

Who said *so?*

Such is the way of the world.

An **adjective** is a descriptive word that qualifies and describes nouns as in:

a *cold* day

a *heavy* shower

Adjectives occur in two main positions in a sentence, before nouns as in the above examples and after verbs like BE, BECOME, GROW, SEEM:

He is *tall*.

He became *angry*.

He grew *fiercer*.

He seems *content*.

Adjectives can thus fill such frames as:

(The) . . . . . men seemed very . . . . . .

(The) . . . . . bread is not very . . . . . .

A **verb** is often defined as a 'doing' word, a word that expresses an action:

John climbed a tree.

a process:

John turned green.

or a state:

John resembles his mother.

Verbs fit into such frames as:

They . . . . . .

Did he . . . . . that?

We might . . . . . .

She is . . . . . ing.

There are two main types of verbs in English, headverbs and auxiliaries. A few examples will illustrate this. In sentences such as:

He hasn't seen me.

He was seen.

He didn't see me.

He might see me tomorrow.

the various forms of SEE are known as the headverb whereas *has, was, did* and *might* are called auxiliary verbs because they help to make more precise the information carried by the headverb. In English it is possible to have a maximum of four auxiliaries in the one verb phrase:

He may have been being followed.

Verbs that can replace 'may' are called 'modals'; HAVE, in this context, is the 'perfective auxiliary'; the first BE is the 'continuative' or 'progressive auxiliary'; and the second BE is used to form 'passives'. There is one other auxiliary in English, often called the 'dummy auxiliary' because it has little meaning but a great deal of structural significance. In the absence of other auxiliaries, DO is used to turn positive statements into negatives or to create questions:

I like him.

I do not (don't) like him.

Do you like him?

Do you not (Don't you) like him?

An **adverb** is used to modify a verb, an adjective, a sentence or another adverb:

John talked *strangely*.

He is *dangerously* ill.

He was, *however*, the best person for the job.

He talked *very* strangely.

Adverbs fit into such test frames as:

He ran very . . . . . .

He is . . . . . intelligent.

A **preposition** is a function word, such as *at*, *by*, *for*, *from*, *to* and *with*. Prepositions are always followed by a noun, a noun phrase or a pronoun.

He talked *to* John.

He arrived *with* another man.

He did it *for* me.

Prepositions fit into such test frames as:

Who went . . . . . John.

Do it . . . . . me.

A **conjunction** is, as its name suggests, a 'joining' word. There are two types of conjunctions: co-ordinating conjunctions such as *and*, *but*, *so*, which join units of equal significance in a sentence:

John *and* Mary ran upstairs.

Give the parcel to John *but* give the money to Mary.

and subordinating conjunctions which join subordinate clauses to a main clause:

He wouldn't tell me *why* he did it.

He said *that* he was tired.

An **exclamation** may be described as an involuntary utterance expressing fear, pain, surprise:

Good lord!

Heavens above!

Oh dear!

The term 'interjection' is often reserved for monosyllabic utterances such as: Oh! Wow! Ouch!

In the written medium, both exclamations and interjections are marked by exclamation marks.

Summary

The foregoing survey is a superficial account of how words function in English. It will guide the student in making decisions about word classes as long as it is remembered that each word must be judged in a specific context. Only context tells us that *any* is a determiner in the first sentence and a pronoun in the second:

Have you any wool?

Have you any?

that *up* is a preposition in the first sentence below, an adverb in the second and a verb in the third:

It ran up the clock.

I can't get up.

He has decided to up his prices.

Exercises

---

1. How many (*a*) orthographic, (*b*) morphological, (*c*) lexical and (*d*) semantic words have we in each of the following lists?

   (1) make, makes, making, made, maiden
   (2) fire, fires, fir, firs, fur
   (3) take, taken, took, taking, takings
   (4) bass (fish), bass (singing voice), bass (tree bark)
   (5) royal, regal, kingly (in the context 'royal/regal/kingly bearing')

2. Expand the following compounds by showing how the two parts are connected. (For example an 'applepie' can be expanded into 'a pie made from apples' and a 'bookcase' can be expanded into 'a case/container for books'.)

   (1) farmyard
   (2) fieldmouse
   (3) girlfriend
   (4) hothouse
   (5) playhouse
   (6) postman
   (7) raincoat
   (8) silkworm
   (9) steamboat
   (10) treehouse

3. Expand the following compounds in the same way as in Exercise 2 and, where possible, say which parts of speech are involved in the compound.

   (1) football
   (2) greenhouse
   (3) handsaw
   (4) highlife

    (5) lambswool
    (6) income
    (7) milkman
    (8) outlook
    (9) scarecrow
 (10) takeaway

4. Decide what part of speech each of the underlined words is.

    (1) Come round to see us.
    (2) All fighting stopped immediately.
    (3) Did you hear what your father said?
    (4) To whom did you give that?
    (5) John and Mary came with their parents.
    (6) Hey! Who told you to do that?
    (7) Seeing is believing.
    (8) He is too happy to go out.
    (9) I'm terribly sorry I took yours.
 (10) What can you see with that?

Chapter 6

Syntax

So FAR THIS STUDY has concentrated on isolated words in the language but now we shall turn to words in combination. British linguists often use the term 'grammar' for the same level of language that is referred to as 'syntax' by many Americans. The differences in the terminology will become clear in Chapter 8 when various models of grammar are examined. For the moment the main emphasis will be on the level of language that examines how words combine into larger units. We shall study only three of these units – the phrase, the clause and the sentence – and we shall provide straightforward, traditional definitions. Different linguists, however, often define terms differently. Structuralists, for example, would label 'sheep', 'that lovely sheep' and 'that sheep are unpredictable' as:

sheep	– word/free morpheme
that lovely sheep	– phrase
that sheep are unpredictable	– clause

whereas transformationalists would call them all noun phrases.

There is value in each approach. The structuralist one concentrates on the formal differences whereas transformationalists concentrate on the functional similarities in that all three can occur in the same slot:

Sheep	can be seen clearly.
That lovely sheep	can be seen clearly.
That sheep are unpredictable	can be seen clearly.

The phrase

For our purpose, we can define a phrase as a group of words which functions as a unit and, with the exception of the verb phrase itself, does not contain a finite verb. Consider this definition by examining a few sentences. In:

The little boy sat in the corner.

we can replace 'the little boy' by 'He' and 'in the corner' by 'there'. Notice that in both examples we replace a number of words by one. Similarly, if we ask: 'Who sat in the corner?' the answer will be 'The little boy' or if we ask: 'Where did he sit?' we will be told 'In the corner'. It is thus clear that certain groups of words have internal coherence in that they function as a unit. We have also said that a phrase does not contain a finite verb, so now we shall look at what a finite verb is.

A finite verb is one that can take as its subject a pronoun such as 'I', 'we', 'he', 'she', 'it', 'they'. Thus we can have:

I see

he sees

they saw

but not:

*I seeing†

*he to see

*we seen

and we can say that the present participle (that is, forms such as 'seeing'), the infinitive (that is, forms such as 'to see') and the past participle (that is, forms such as 'seen') are non-finite verb forms. Only non-finite verb forms can occur in phrases:

Bending low, he walked awkwardly into the small room.

Seen from this angle, the mountains look blue.

There are five commonly occurring types of phrase in English: noun phrases, adjective phrases, verb phrases, adverb phrases and preposition phrases.

1. A **noun phrase** is a group of words with a noun as its headword. There can be up to three noun phrases in a simple sentence, as the underlined units in the following simple sentences show:

      1   2   3

The young man threw the old dog a bone.

     1   2   3

That rich man will build his eldest daughter a fine house.

2. An **adjective phrase** is a group of words which modifies a noun. Like adjectives, these words can be either attributive (that is, usually preceding but occasionally following a noun):

The child, laughing happily, ran out of the house.

That utterly fascinating novel has been banned.

†An asterisk *before* an utterance indicates that the utterance is unacceptable in normal conditions.

or predicative (that is, following a verb):

The letter was <u>unbelievably rude</u>.

He seemed <u>extremely pleasant</u>.

3. A **verb phrase** is a group of words with a verb as headword. Verb phrases can be either finite:

He <u>has been singing</u>.

or non-finite:

<u>to have sung</u>

A simple sentence can have only one finite verb phrase:

He <u>may be following</u> us.

but a complex sentence may have several finite verb phrases:

When he <u>was invited</u> to give a lecture, he <u>was told</u> that all reasonable expenses <u>would be refunded</u>.

4. An **adverb phrase** is a group of words which functions like an adverb; it often plays the role of telling us when, where, why or how an event occurred:

We are expecting him to come <u>next year</u>.

He <u>almost always</u> arrives on time.

He ran <u>very quickly</u>.

5. A **preposition phrase** is a group of words that begins with a preposition:

He arrived <u>by plane</u>.

Do you know that man <u>with the scar</u>?

We are <u>on very good terms</u>.

A number of modern linguists use the term 'phrase' in a slightly different way to that described above. They compare such sentences as:

The young man has arrived.

and:

He arrived.

pointing out that 'he' functions in exactly the same way as 'the young man' and 'arrived' in exactly the same way as 'has arrived'. Concentrating on the similarity of function, they define a noun phrase, for example, as 'a word or group of words which can function as a subject, object or complement in a sentence':

The young man came in/He came in.

The young man defended his mother/He defended her.

The answer was '400 hours'/The answer was this.

Similarly, a verb phrase is a word or group of words which can function as a predicate in a sentence:

He arrived at two.　　He will arrive at two.

Both uses have value. A student must be aware of the different values attached to the same word but must also be consistent in his own use.

The clause

A clause is a group of words which contains a finite verb but which cannot occur in isolation, that is, a clause constitutes only part of a sentence. In each complex sentence, we have at least two clauses: a main clause (that is, a clause that is most like a simple sentence) and at least one subordinate or dependent clause. In the following examples, the main clauses are underlined:

He believed that the earth was round.

He arrived as the clock was striking.

The following types of subordinate clause are found:

1. A **noun clause** is a group of words containing a finite verb and functioning like a noun:

He said that he was tired.

What you said was not true.

The fact that the earth moves round the sun is well known.

Noun clauses can often be replaced by pronouns:

He said this.

When you are in doubt about how a clause functions in a sentence, you should see what can be substituted for it. All the following possibilities are acceptable:

I shall always remember	John.
	him.
	his kindness.
	what John has done.

Thus, pronouns, nouns and noun phrases can usually be substituted for noun clauses.

2. An **adjective clause** is often called a 'relative clause' because it usually relates back to a noun whose meaning it modifies:

The dog <u>which won the competition</u> is an alsatian.

The man <u>who taught my brother French</u> is now the headmaster.

The girl <u>whom we met on holiday</u> is coming to see us next week.

When an adjective/relative clause begins with 'that/which/whom' and is followed by a subject, the subordinator can be omitted:

The book <u>(that) John bought</u> is missing.

The coat <u>(which) she wore</u> is red.

The man <u>(whom) we met</u> was my uncle.

There is virtually no difference in meaning between:

The book which I bought . . . . . .

and:

The book that I bought . . . . . .

or:

The book I bought . . . . . .

although the third is the least formal and so the most likely to occur in spontaneous speech.

Occasionally an adjective clause can begin with 'when':

I remember the day <u>when we won the cup</u>.

or 'where':

The town <u>where they met</u> was called Scarborough.

It is usually easy to decide whether a 'when/where' clause is adjectival or adverbial. If the 'when' can be replaced by 'on which' and the 'where' by 'in which/at which' we are dealing with adjective clauses.

3. An **adverbial clause** functions like an adverb in giving information about when, where, why, how or if an action occurred:

<u>When he arrived</u> we were all sleeping.

Put it <u>where we can all see it</u>.

They won the match <u>because they were the best players</u>.

He put it away as <u>quietly as he could</u>.

<u>If you want any more</u> you'll have to get it yourself.

Adverbial clauses are perhaps the most frequently used clauses in the language and, like adverbs, they are often mobile:

When he arrived we were all sleeping.

We were all sleeping when he arrived.

A number of modern linguists use the term 'clause' somewhat differently to the above classification. They call units containing a finite verb 'finite clauses' and units containing non-finite verb forms such as 'to see', 'seeing' and 'seen', 'non-finite clauses'. A few examples will illustrate their usage. In the following sentences:

He went to Paris because he wanted a rest.

He went to Paris to have a rest.

both underlined units tell us why he went to Paris but only the first one contains a finite verb. Similarly with:

When he heard the results he went home.

On hearing the results he went home.

and:

If it is looked at from this angle the colours seem to change.

Looked at from this angle the colours seem to change.

the underlined units function in similar ways, being distinguished mainly by the fact that the first examples contain finite verbs and the second examples non-finite verbs. Linguists who concentrate on the formal distinction, that is, the occurrence or non-occurrence of a finite verb in a unit, classify such units as clauses and phrases respectively. Those who concentrate on the functional similarities classify both these units as clauses, distinguishing between them in terms of whether the verb used is finite or non-finite. Thus all linguists will agree that the underlined units in the following sentences function as subjects:

His behaviour is understandable.

To behave in this way is understandable.

Whatever he does is understandable.

but they will classify these subjects according to their preferred model. What is important is to be consistent in one's use of terminology.

The sentence

In 1952 C. C. Fries (see Bibliography) examined over two hundred definitions of 'sentence' in the hope of finding the most useful. He discovered that, as with so many grammatical units, it is easier to show what they look like than to say what they are. Thus the following are sentences:

The man died.

The dog chased the cat.

The girl is a good student.

That child is very tall.

The boy ran up the hill.

They can exist independently, do not rely on any other unit and can be interpreted without reference to any other piece of language. Fries decided that the most workable definition of sentence was the one that had been provided by Bloomfield in 1933 (see Bibliography), according to which:

Each sentence is an independent linguistic form, not included by virtue of any grammatical construction in any larger linguistic form.

All the above examples fit this definition. 'The man died', for example, is independent in a way that 'when the man died' is not. This clause depends on such a construction as:

They were all very sad (when the man died).

An even simpler categorisation of 'sentence' can be applied to the written medium in that we can define a sentence as 'that linguistic unit which begins with a capital letter and ends with a full stop'. Both these definitions of 'sentence' are useful but it will be worth our while to study further both the types of sentences that occur in English and their internal construction.

Sentences can be divided into four sub-types:

1. **Declarative sentences** make statements or assertions:

I shall arrive at three.

You are not the only applicant.

Peace has its victories.

We must not forget that date.

2. **Imperative sentences** give orders, make requests and usually have no overt subject:

Come here.

Don't do that.

Try to help.

Don't walk on the grass.

3. **Interrogative sentences** ask questions:

Did you see your brother yesterday?

Can't you hear that awful noise?

When did he arrive?

Why don't they play cricket here?

You will notice that there are two types of interrogative question, those which expect the answer '*yes*' or '*no*':

Can you sing?

Are you going to the wedding?

and those which begin with the question words *what?*, *where?*, *which?*, *who?*, *whom?*, *why?*, or *how?* and which expect an answer other than *yes* or *no*.

4. **Exclamatory sentences** are used to express surprise, alarm, indignation or a strong opinion. They are differentiated from other sentences by taking an exclamation mark:

He's going to win!

You can't be serious!

What a fool I was!

I've never heard such rubbish in all my life!

Sentences can also be classified as being either *major* or *minor*. All the examples above are major in that they contain finite verbs. Minor sentences do not contain finite verbs and they are frequently found in colloquial speech:

Got a match?

Not likely!

Just a minute!

in proverbial utterances:

Out of sight, out of mind.

In for a penny, in for a pound.

and in advertising:

Always ahead of the times.

The cheapest and best.

Apart from the above categorisations of sentences, we often find it useful to distinguish between sentences which are 'simple', 'compound' or 'complex'.

Simple sentences contain only one finite verb:

Water <u>boils</u> at 100° centigrade.

You <u>must</u> not <u>say</u> such things.

The finite verb may be composed of up to four auxiliaries plus a headverb:

He <u>may have been being followed</u> all the time.

and may be interrupted by a negative or an adverb:

He <u>was</u> never <u>seen</u> again.

We <u>can</u> hardly <u>ask</u> them for any more.

The term 'simple' refers to the fact that the sentence contains only one finite verb. It does *not* imply that the sentence is easy to understand. The following sentence, for example, is simple in structure but semantically it is quite difficult:

Quangos *are* quasi-autonomous, non-governmental organisations.

Compound sentences consist of two or more simple sentences linked by the co-ordinating conjunctions *and, but, so, either . . . or, neither . . . nor, or, then* and *yet*:

He ran out and (he) fell over the suitcase.

She arrived at nine, went up to her room and did not come down until noon.

He could neither eat nor sleep.

In compound sentences, the shared elements in the conjoined simple sentences can be elided:

You may go in and (you may) talk to him for five minutes.

Complex sentences consist of one simple sentence and one or more subordinate (or dependent) clauses. In the following sentence:

She became queen when her father died because she was the eldest child.

we have one main clause:

She became queen

and two subordinate clauses:

when her father died

and:

because she was the eldest child.

You will notice that each clause has a finite verb, 'became', 'died' and 'was' in the example above, and that each subordinate clause begins with a subordinating conjunction. The commonest subordinating conjunctions in English are:

after:	She washed the dishes after she had cooked the meal.
although/though:	Although they were poor, they were honest.
as:	As John says, it's time to go.
as . . . (as):	He is as tall as his father was.
because:	He left the town because he did not like crowds.
before:	He arrived before we did.
if:	If you try hard you will certainly succeed.
since:	I have not seen him since we left grammar school.
until/till:	He worried about everything until his daughter arrived.
when:	Time passes quickly when you are happy.
where:	He built his home where his ancestors had lived.
whether . . . or not:	John is the best runner whether he knows it or not.
which/that:	This is the house which/that Jack built.
while:	Do not cross the tracks while the lights are red.

Subordinate clauses are characterised by the fact that they cannot occur alone. They depend on a main clause. In some modern descriptions, subordinate clauses are called 'embedded sentences' because they resemble simple sentences but are modified so as to fit into other constructions. We can have, for example, the two simple sentences:

The man arrived late.

and:

The man wore a large hat.

The second is embedded in the first when we transform the two simple sentences into the complex one:

The man who wore a large hat arrived late.

Compound-complex sentences are, as their name suggests, a combination of complex sentences joined by co-ordinating conjunctions:

I saw him when he arrived the first time but I didn't see him when he came again.

We have looked at the types of sentences that can occur and will now focus on the internal structure of a sentence. The basic pattern of the simple English sentence is:

(Adjunct) (Subject) Predicate (Object) (Complement) (Adjunct)

usually given as:

(A) (S) P (O) (C) (A)

where only the predicate is essential and where the adjunct is mobile. A few simple examples will show how the formula works.

Such sentences as:

The man disappeared.

The poor young woman died.

divide into two parts, a noun part:

The man

The poor young woman

and a verb part:

disappeared

died

We call the noun part a 'subject' and the verb part a 'predicate'. We know that the subject is a unit because we can substitute 'he' for 'the man' and 'she' for 'the poor young woman'. The verb part can usually be retrieved by asking such questions as 'what did he do?/what has he done?' and omitting the pronoun in the answer. Notice that if our first sentence had been:

The man has disappeared.

our question would retrieve the whole predicate, in this case 'has disappeared'.

In the sentences:

The man disappeared yesterday.

Quite suddenly the man disappeared.

the underlined segments are called 'adjuncts' because they can usually be deleted without causing grammatical loss. (Their removal would, of course, result in loss of information.) These adjuncts are usually quite mobile:

Suddenly the man disappeared.

The man suddenly disappeared.

The man disappeared suddenly.

If we take a different type of sentence:

John won't eat his breakfast.

we see that it splits up into three parts: the subject 'John', the predicate 'won't eat' and the object 'his breakfast'. The object resembles the subject in that it is noun-like, but there are three main differences:

(1) The subject normally precedes the predicate. The object normally follows the predicate.
(2) The subject can usually be retrieved by putting *who* or *what* before the predicate, 'Who won't eat his breakfast?' produces the answer 'John', the subject. The object can be retrieved by putting 'whom' or 'what' after the predicate: 'John won't eat what?' produces the answer 'his breakfast', the object.
(3) When subjects and objects are replaced by pronouns, there is often a different pronoun for the two positions:

John hit Peter.   He hit him.

Mary hit Betty.   She hit her.

John and Mary hit Peter and Betty.   They hit them.

Adjuncts can occur in most sentences:

Usually John won't eat his breakfast.

John won't eat his breakfast usually.

Looking now at such sentences as:

John is a fine teacher.   Mary is becoming an excellent athlete.

we see that we again have three parts, but there is a fundamental difference between these sentences and sentences of the type Subject Predicate Object in that 'John' = 'a fine teacher' and 'Mary' = 'an excellent athlete'. Such sentences always involve such verbs as BE, BECOME, SEEM and APPEAR, and GROW when they are used in such constructions as:

He appeared the best choice.   He grew weary.

These verbs take 'complements' and the complements can be a noun phrase:

He was a first-class sportsman.

an adjective:

She is becoming insolent.

a preposition + a noun phrase:

He was in the bus.

and occasionally an adverb:

The fire is out.

The complements above are called 'subject complements' because they provide information on the subjects. We can also have 'object complements' as in:

They elected John President.

John called his son Peter.

Again, you will notice that the object 'John' is the same as 'President' and 'his son' as 'Peter'. Sentences involving complements can also have adjuncts:

John was a candidate yesterday.

They elected John President yesterday.

We can summarise the above data with examples as follows:

P	Go.
PA	Go quietly.
SP	John slept.
SPA	John slept quietly.
PO	Eat your breakfast.
SPO	John ate his breakfast.
SPOA	John ate his breakfast quickly.
SPC	John is a fool.
ASPC	At times John is a fool.
SPOC	John called his brother a fool.
SAPOC	John often called his brother a fool.

In our examination of sentence patterns, four operations will prove useful. They are *insertion*, *deletion*, *substitution* and *transposition* (also called *permutation*). We can illustrate these operations as follows:

Insertion: This would involve changing such a sentence as:

The child is clever.

into:

The little child is exceptionally clever.

Deletion: In the sentence:

The tall man saw him last Friday.

we can delete the adjective 'tall' and the adjunct 'last Friday' leaving the grammatically acceptable:

The man saw him.

Substitution: In such sentences as:

The young man visited his mother.

we can substitute pronouns for both subject and object:

He visited her.

Often too, auxiliary verbs can replace verb phrases:

He might have come, mightn't he?

where 'mightn't he' substitutes for 'might he not have come'.

Transposition: This involves the mobility of sentence constituents and we have already seen how adjuncts can be transposed/moved from one part of a sentence to another. Other sentence constituents are less mobile, but occasionally, for effect, an object may precede both subject and predicate:

Three men I saw.

However, such a sentence is much less usual than 'I saw three men'.

Above the sentence

So far our analysis has been confined to the level of the sentence or below, yet sentences in a coherent piece of prose interact, as the following example illustrates:

Thomas Gainsborough, who was to become one of the greatest English painters, was born in 1727 in Sudbury in Suffolk. As a boy he seemed interested in only drawing and sketching. One day he saw a man robbing an orchard. Young Gainsborough made a sketch of the man and it was so good that the robber was recognised from it and arrested. At fifteen he was sent to London to study art. He returned to Sudbury when he was eighteen and began painting portraits. He got married at nineteen. In 1760 he went to Bath, then a very fashionable resort.

The cohesion of the above text depends on a number of factors including:

(1) **consistency of vocabulary**: many items belong to the semantic field of art, for example, painters, drawing, sketching, sketch, art, painting, portraits; and time is frequently indicated, for example 1727, as a boy, one day, at fifteen, eighteen, nineteen, 1760.

(2) **consistency of time references**: the entire passage is in the past and there are no sudden switches to the present or the future.

(3) **linkage**: looking closely at the text we see that there are a number of links between the sentences. In particular, we might mention: he. . . he. . . a man. . . the man. . . it. . . it. . . he. . . He. . . he. . . He. . . he. . . then

Linkage is a means of interrelating syntactically complete sentences and there are eight main types of linkage apart from consistency of vocabulary. These are:

(i) units that suggest addition, for example: as well as, furthermore, in addition, together with

(ii) units which suggest alternatives, for example: either . . . or, on the other hand, otherwise

(iii) units which suggest sequences, for example: first, to begin with, to conclude, and then

(iv) units which suggest cause and effect, for example: because, hence, so, therefore

(v) units which suggest conditions, for example: as long as, if, providing, on condition that, unless

(vi) units which suggest time, for example: afterwards, earlier, later, on another occasion

(vii) noun substitutes, for example: demonstrative pronouns, personal pronouns, the former, the latter

(viii) verb substitutes, for example: auxiliary verbs and DO.

Grammatical, acceptable, interpretable

It is perhaps appropriate to consider the meanings of these three words as they apply to language. A piece of language is 'grammatical' if it does not break any of the rules of the standard language. Thus:

The cat died.

is grammatical as is:

The cat that the dog chased died.

and so is:

The cat that the dog that the man hit chased died.

Most native speakers would not, however, accept the third sentence. It is certainly grammatical in that all we have done is add one adjective clause that describes the dog. The result, however, is three consecutive verbs and this is unacceptable. It is unacceptable *in form* rather than in content as is clear if we look at an acceptable version of the above sentence:

This is the man that hit the dog that chased the cat that died.

As soon as the adjective clauses occur at the end of the sentence we can accept any number of them. When they are embedded within a sentence, most people cannot accept more than two adjective clauses.

If we now look at sentences which are ambiguous, we find a second type of unacceptability. A sentence such as:

Their designs were unacceptable.

cannot, out of context, be interpreted as having one meaning. Here 'designs' could mean either 'drawings' or 'intentions'. When the ambiguity resides in the word it is called 'lexical ambiguity' and this is a common feature of English and of many other languages. At its most extreme, we can have a word like 'cleave' which can mean both 'adhere to/cling to' and also 'open up/separate'. With most words, however, the meanings are related as when 'chip' can refer to a small piece of wood, of potato or of silicon. As well as lexical ambiguity, we have syntactic ambiguity where a structure is capable of more than one interpretation. In English, the structure:

V_{ing} + noun

is the most frequent cause of syntactic ambiguity.

Visiting relatives can cause problems.

is ambiguous because it can mean both:

Relatives who visit us can cause problems

and:

When we visit relatives there can be problems.

Headlines in newspapers are a common source of syntactic ambiguity partly because of the need for compression. The following recent headline, for example:

PAY CUTS PROBLEMS

is capable of two contradictory interpretations: 'The pay settlement will reduce problems' and 'Here are the problems associated with cuts in pay'.

Sentences involving ambiguity thus lead to problems of interpretation. In speech or in continuous prose such ambiguities are rarely noticed because the context of situation or the use of intonation and stress makes one interpretation most probable. In isolation, however, in the written medium, a unique interpretation is often impossible.

Samples of non-standard English are usually interpretable although they are ungrammatical according to the rules of the standard language. If a speaker, for example, says:

*I seen him yesterday.

most listeners have no problem interpreting this. Similarly, few would experience problems in interpreting:

*Pass me them boots.

*He did it for to please his friend.

Thus interpretability does not depend directly on grammaticality.

Where the sample of language deliberately frustrates the expectations of a language user, as when an inanimate noun is made to collocate with a verb that needs an animate subject, as in:

*Gentleness admired the view.

*Happiness broke its leg.

then the result will be neither grammatical, nor acceptable, nor interpretable.

We should add that what has been called 'poetic licence' allows poets to exploit language in ways which would be unacceptable in normal circumstances. The American poet e e cummings (who refused to use capital letters or full stops after his initials) produced such lines as:

anyone lived in a pretty how town

four fleet does at a gold valley

the famished arrow sang before

which are certainly not intelligible out of context. And when the linguist, Noam Chomsky, created a sentence which deliberately frustrated our expectations:

Colourless green ideas sleep furiously.

(colourless cannot be green; ideas cannot be green; ideas cannot sleep; sleeping is a passive experience) several poets insisted that, for them, the sentence was acceptable.

Summary

We have now looked at the syntax of the language and seen the flexibility that can be exploited by users of English. It is worth remembering that complex structures are not necessarily a feature of good style and also that effective communication relies on a structure being grammatical, acceptable and interpretable.

Exercises

---

1. Pick out and classify the phrases in the following sentences. (EXAMPLE: 'The young boy will be running very fast'. Here we have three phrases: a noun phrase 'The young boy', a verb phrase 'will be running' and an adverb phrase 'very fast'.)

   (1) Please send me three boxes of biscuits on the 14th of July.
   (2) All the children seemed extremely happy.
   (3) She couldn't go to the fête because of her bad cold.
   (4) To have played football for Manchester United was his greatest achievement.
   (5) The boy will have arrived in Spain by this time.

2. Pick out the noun clauses in the following sentences and say whether they function as subjects, objects or complements.

   (1) She supposed that they would have enough money.
   (2) What we heard was a tissue of lies.
   (3) When confronted by the facts, he became what one might describe as agitated.
   (4) That is all I can remember.
   (5) 'Who was she?' was of course the first question that everyone asked.

3. Write down all the clauses in the following sentences saying (*a*) whether they are main or subordinate clauses and (*b*) what type of subordinate clause has been used.

   (1) I shall always remember what you said.
   (2) When we arrived everyone was asleep.
   (3) It was what everyone had feared.
   (4) He arrived on the very day when we were celebrating your birthday.
   (5) The hat which I bought was the wrong colour.

4. Turn the following sentences into (*a*) imperatives and (*b*) interrogatives.

(1) He will come at eight o'clock.
(2) She doesn't do that.
(3) She tries to help.
(4) He doesn't play cricket.
(5) You can't be serious!

5. Classify each of the following sentences according to whether they
are (*a*) major or minor and (*b*) simple, complex or compound.

(1) Not on your life!
(2) What will we do if they don't turn up?
(3) One man one vote.
(4) He ran into the room, picked up his coat and ran out again.
(5) Often it is impossible to say whether they are telling the truth or
not.
(6) The man whom we met at the party and whom we later invited
home has just rung to say he can't come tonight.
(7) Anything goes!
(8) The whitest wash and the sweetest-smelling wash too!
(9) Don't count your chickens before they are hatched.
(10) Out of sight out of mind.

6. Select any short passage of either prose or poetry and list *all* the
ways in which the sentences are linked.

Chapter 7

Semantics

WE HAVE ALREADY COME ACROSS the word 'semantic' in Chapter 5 when we examined the different connotations of 'word'. Semantics refers to meaning and meaning is so intangible that one group of linguists, the structuralists, preferred not to deal with it or rely on it at all. To illustrate what we mean by the intangible quality of 'meaning', think of such words as 'beauty', 'goodness', 'love'; it would be hard to find two people who agree absolutely on what each of these words implies. A person may seem good to one onlooker and a hypocrite to another. Similarly, we all think we know what we mean by 'boy' and 'man', but at what age does a boy cease to be a boy? at thirteen? fifteen? eighteen? twenty-one? Meaning is a variable and not to be taken for granted.

Under the subject of semantics we shall deal with the following areas of interest:

(1) the fact that a word can have more than one meaning, for example *ball* can be both a dance and a round object for bouncing
(2) the fact that different words appear to have the same meaning, for example 'regal' and 'royal' or 'big' and 'large'
(3) the fact that some words can be analysed into components such as adult, female, for example *mare* implies both adult and female as well as horse
(4) the fact that some words seem to have opposites, for example 'long' and 'short', 'good' and 'bad' but not 'desk' or 'table'
(5) the fact that the meanings of some words are included in the meaning of others, for example the meaning of 'vegetable' is included in that of 'potato' and the meaning of 'tree' is included in that of 'elm'
(6) the fact that certain combinations of words have meanings which are very different from the combination of their separate meanings, for example the meanings of 'pass' plus the meanings of 'on' do not add up to the meaning of 'die' although that is what 'pass on' can mean.

Polysemy

The same morphological word may have a range of different meanings as a glance at any dictionary will reveal. Polysemy, meaning 'many meanings', is the name given to the study of this particular phenomenon. In a dictionary entry for any given word the meanings are listed in a particular order with the central meaning given first, followed by the most closely related meanings and with metaphorical extensions coming last. If we look up the word 'star', for example, in the *Concise Oxford Dictionary*, we find the meanings:

(1) celestial body
(2) thing suggesting star by its shape, especially a figure or object with radiating points
(3) (in card game) additional life bought by player whose lives are lost
(4) principal actor or actress in a company

In theory, the idea of words having several meanings is straightforward; in practice there are problems, especially in relation to drawing boundary lines between words. It is not always easy to decide when a meaning has become so different from its original meaning that it deserves to be treated like a new word. The *Concise Oxford Dictionary*, for example, lists 'pupil' as having two meanings:

(1) one who is taught by another, scholar
(2) circular opening in centre of iris of eye regulating passage of light to the retina

Many speakers of English, however, regard these as two different words. Stated simply, the essential problem is that it is not always easy or even possible to be certain whether we are dealing with polysemy, that is, one word with several meanings, or homonymy, that is, several words with the same form.

Normally dictionaries decide between polysemy and homonymy by referring to etymology (the origins and history of a word) when this is known, but even this rule is not foolproof because, on occasions, etymologically related words may have different spellings as in the case of 'flower' and 'flour'. The simplest solution is to seek a core of meaning and any homonymous items sharing the core of meaning should be classified as polysemous.

The phenomenon of polysemy is not restricted to full words in English. Multiplicity of meaning is a very general characteristic of language and is found in prefixes as well as full words. Let us take 'un' for example. When it prefixes a verb, it usually means 'reverse the action of the verb': undo, unpack, untie, unzip. When 'un' precedes a noun to form a verb, it can mean 'deprive of this noun': 'unhorse', 'unman' (that is, deprive of manly qualities). This usage is rare in English now but previously words like 'unbishop', 'unduke', 'unking', 'unlord' occurred. When 'un' precedes an adjective, it can mean 'the opposite of': 'unfair', 'ungracious', 'unkind', 'untrue'.

Synonymy

Most people think of 'synonymy' as implying 'having the same meaning' but it is easy to show that synonymy is always partial, never complete. 'Tall' and 'high' are usually given as synonyms but whilst we can have both:

a tall building

and:

a high building

we cannot have both:

a tall boy

and:

*a high boy

We can best define synonymy by saying that it is the relationship in which two or more words are in free variation in all or most contexts. The closest we come to absolute synonymy is when the synonyms belong to different dialects as with:

British usage	*US usage*
autumn	fall
estate agent	realtor
pavement	sidewalk

but even here the choice of one term rather than another indicates a regional preference. As well as regionally marked synonyms, we find synonyms which differ stylistically, in that one term may be more formal than another:

die	pass on/over	kick the bucket	decease
steal	relieve one of	pinch/half inch	purloin
smell	odour	stink/pong	effluvium

And, as the above items also illustrate, items which are cognitively synonymous may arouse very different emotional responses, the A list below implying less approval than the B list:

A	*B*
conceal	hide
politician	statesman
stubborn	resolute

Total synonymy, that is, the coincidence of cognitive, emotive and stylistic identity, is more of an ideal than a reality. In addition, the choice of one word rather than its synonym can have an effect on the words and phrases than can co-occur with it. Let us illustrate this briefly by listing dictionary synonyms for 'put up with' and 'noise':

put up with	*noise*
bear	clamour
brook	din
endure	disturbance
stand	sound level
tolerate	

All the verbs can collocate with 'such noise' although 'brook' is more likely to occur with words like 'impertinence', 'offhandedness' or 'rudeness'. As soon as we try to substitute 'clamour' for 'noise' we meet our first problem. We can say:

I can't put up with such noise.

but for most native speakers:

I can't put up with such clamour.

is unacceptable. In addition, if we substitute 'din' we need to include an indefinite article 'such a din', and the same applies to 'racket'. What is being stressed here is the fact that items collocate and interact. We must take levels of formality into account in selecting synonyms.

Antonymy

This is the general term applied to the sense relation involving oppositeness of meaning. For our purposes, it will be convenient to distinguish three types of 'oppositeness', namely (1) implicitly graded antonyms, (2) complementarity and (3) converseness.

(1) **Implicitly graded antonyms** refer to pairs of items such as 'big' and 'small', 'good' and 'bad', 'young' and 'old'. In other words, 'big', 'good' and 'young' can only be interpreted in terms of being 'bigger', 'better' or 'younger' than something which is established as the norm for the comparison. Thus, when we say that one fly is bigger than another, we imply that 'big' is to be understood in the context of flies. This accounts for the apparent paradox of a 'big fly' being smaller than a 'small dog' because 'small' in the latter context means 'small when compared with other dogs'.

In English, the larger item of the pair is the unmarked or neutral member. Thus we can ask:

How big is it?
How old is he?
How wide is the river?

without implying that the subject is either 'big', 'old' or 'wide'. Such questions are unbiased or open with regard to the expectations of the enquirer. On the other hand, to ask:

How small is it?

does prejudge the matter, claiming that it is indeed small. There is nothing universal about the larger member of the pair being the neutral member although in many societies this seems to be the case. In Japanese, for example, one would ask the equivalent of:

How thin is it?

when an English speaker would have to ask:

How thick is it?

(2) **Complementarity** refers to the existence of such pairs as 'male' and 'female'. It is characteristic of such pairs that the denial of one implies the assertion of the other. Thus if one is not male, then one is certainly female. Notice the difference between graded antonyms of the 'good'/'bad' type and complementary pairs. To say:

John is not single.

implies:

John is married.

but to say:

John is not bad.

does not imply:

John is good.

In certain contexts, the following can be complementary pairs:

food	drink
land	sea
transitive	intransitive
warmblooded	coldblooded

Related to complementary sets are sets of terms like colours or numbers where the assertion of one member implies the negation of all the others. Thus, if we have a set such as: green, yellow, brown, red, blue, to say:

This is green.

implies that it is not yellow, brown, red or blue. In a two-term set such as (male, female), the assertion of male implies the denial of the only other term in the set. Such terms, as well as being described as 'complementary', are often referred to as 'incompatible'.

(3) **Converseness** is the relationship that holds between such related pairs of sentences as:

John sold it to me.

and:

I bought it from John.

where SELL and BUY are in a converse relationship. English has a number of conversely related verbs and so sentence converseness is a common phenomenon:

John lent the money to Peter.

Peter borrowed the money from John.

Other frequently occurring converse verbs include:

buy and sell

push and pull

command and serve

give and take

hire out and hire

lease and rent

teach and learn

Occasionally, the same verb can be used in the conversely related pair of sentences as in:

John rented the house to Peter.

Peter rented the house from John.

and also:

John married Mary.

and:

Mary married John.

Sometimes, in English, we can find converse nouns corresponding to converse verbs:

command	serve	master	servant
teach	learn	teacher	pupil
treat	consult	doctor	patient

Hyponymy

Hyponymy is related to complementarity and incompatibility. Whereas the relationship of implicit denial is called incompatibility, the relationship of implicit inclusion is called hyponymy. This relationship is easy to demonstrate. The colour 'red', for example, includes or comprehends the colours 'scarlet' and 'vermilion' just as the term 'flower' includes 'daisy', 'forget-me-not' and 'rose'. The including term in our latter example 'flower' is known as the 'superordinate term' and the included items are known as 'co-hyponyms'. The assertion of a hyponym:

This is a rose.

implies the assertion of the superordinate:

This is a flower.

but the assertion of the superordinate does not automatically imply one specific hyponym. We can thus say that the implicational nature of hyponymy is unilateral or works one way only.

One of the most useful features of the principle of hyponymy is that it allows us to be as general or as specific as a particular linguistic occasion warrants, as can be seen from the following hierarchies:

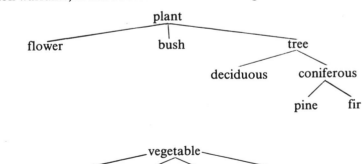

Often these hierarchical diagrams are called 'taxonomies'. With each downward step we encounter terms of more specific meaning.

Hyponymy is a recently invented method of indicating the relationships that can exist between words. Occasionally, items have to be put into a context to see whether their relationships can best be illustrated by means of one classification rather than another. 'Black' and 'white' are co-hyponyms when considered as colours but they can be complementary in discussions about race, draughts and piano keys.

Idioms

An idiom is a group of words whose meaning cannot be explained in terms of the habitual meanings of the words that make up the piece of language. Thus 'fly off the handle' which means 'lose one's temper' cannot be understood in terms of the meanings of 'fly', 'off' or 'handle'. Idioms involve the non-literal use of language and they can be categorised as follows:

(1) *alliterative comparisons*:

> dead as a dodo
>
> fit as a fiddle
>
> good as gold

(2) *noun phrases*:

> a blind alley (route that leads nowhere, a false trail)
>
> a close shave (a narrow escape)
>
> a red letter day (a day that will never be forgotten)

(3) *preposition phrases*:

> at sixes and sevens (unable/unwilling to agree)
>
> by hook or by crook (by whatever methods prove necessary)
>
> in for a penny, in for a pound ('I'm involved irrespective of cost')

(4) *verb + noun phrase*:

> kick the bucket (die)
>
> pop your clogs (die)
>
> spill the beans (reveal a secret)

(5) *verb + preposition phrase*:

> be in clover (be exceptionally comfortable)
>
> be in the doghouse (be in disgrace)
>
> be between a rock and a hard place (have no room for manoeuvre)

(6) *verb + adverb*:

  give in (yield)

  put down (kill)

  take to (like)

Idioms range from the semi-transparent where either the meaning can be interpreted in terms of metaphor:

  clip someone's wings (reduce someone's mobility)

or because one part of the idiomatic phrase is used literally:

  run up a bill

to the totally opaque:

  go bananas (lose one's temper)

They tend to be relatively fixed with regard to number:

  spill the beans *and not* *spill the bean

the use of determiners:

  a dead duck *and not* *the/that dead duck

the use of comparatives and superlatives:

  good as gold *and not* *better than gold

  red tape *and not* *reddest tape

word order:

  hale and hearty *and not* *hearty and hale

the use of passives:

  They buried the hatchet *and not* *The hatchet was buried

  He spilt the beans *and not* *The beans were spilt

There is a tendency for the more transparent idioms to allow some change:

  run up a bill *and* run up an enormous bill

but:

  kick the bucket *and not* *kick the enormous bucket

and there is a marked tendency for a few colours – black, blue, green, red and white – to be used idiomatically:

  blackmail   a blue moon   a red herring   a white elephant

Idioms differ according to region and according to formality. They are more frequently found in speech than in writing and, because they are both hackneyed and imprecise, they are best avoided in formal contexts. Idioms are a marked example of non-literal use of language and, although they occur in all languages, they can rarely be translated from one language to another.

Summary

Meaning is not an easy concept to deal with partly because we are dealing with abstractions (one person's idea of 'goodness' may differ radically from another's), with mobility ('silly' used to mean 'holy' and 'regiment' used to mean 'government'), with difference of opinion (when, for example, does a hill become a mountain or a sea become an ocean?) and with distinctions essential in one language but not in another (the English only need one word for 'sand' but Arabs need many more). To meet some of these problems linguists have tried to deal with sense relations, that is, with the relationships that exist within a specific language, in terms of similarity (synonymy), differences (antonymy), related sets (complementarity and hyponymy) and the non-literal use of language (idiom). They examine the lexicon in terms of systems in which individual words depend for their meaning on being opposed to other items in a set. 'Good' can only be fully understood by being opposed to 'bad' or 'better' or 'worse'. In addition, qualitative adjectives can only be understood in terms of an implied norm. 'Good' for example can be used to modify:

behaviour

looks

mood

We can even talk about a 'good liar' because, in each case, 'good' is related to a standard relevant to behaviour, looks, moods and liars. Meaning is not 'given' and is never absolute.

Exercises

---

1. Offer synonyms for the underlined words in the following sentences:
    (1) We saw a tiny child.
    (2) He was praised for his kingly bearing.
    (3) He hid the news from his mother and father.
    (4) He was overcome by the nasty effluvium.
    (5) Indicate the route to my abode.
    (6) He could not tolerate the noise.

(7) He always referred to himself as a labourer.
(8) She lit it.
(9) He always nods off as soon as he sits by the fire.
(10) Please don't meddle with my possessions again.

2. Select the most appropriate antonyms for the underlined items in the following sentences:

   (1) It was the smallest elephant I had ever seen.
   (2) My coffee is cold.
   (3) My feet are cold.
   (4) My house is cold.
   (5) He has dark hair.
   (6) He gave me a dark look.
   (7) The sky is becoming very dark.
   (8) He disappeared.
   (9) We arrived at noon.
   (10) It was a very wide river.

3. Put the following lists into taxonomic hierarchies:

   (1) rose, plant, tea-rose, dog-rose, flower, daisy
   (2) tea, coffee, beverage, milk, black coffee, sugared coffee
   (3) cold-blooded animals, warm-blooded animals, animals, crocodiles, birds, fish, whales

4. Examine the following sentences carefully and try to establish a hierarchy of the verbs used. (Put the most general verb at the top.)

   (1) He rushed down the road.
   (2) He went down the road.
   (3) He walked down the road.
   (4) He strolled down the road.
   (5) He ran down the road.

Which of the above verbs are mutually exclusive? That is, if we assert one verb like 'run' do we automatically deny another verb?

5. Complete the following idioms:

   (1) as right as . . . . .
   (2) a . . . . . moon
   (3) by the skin of his . . . . .
   (4) burn the . . . . . at both ends
   (5) bark up the wrong . . . . .
   (6) cry for the . . . . .
   (7) go on a wild . . . . . chase
   (8) bite the . . . . .
   (9) keep a . . . . . profile
   (10) get to the . . . . . gritty

Chapter 8

Linguistic schools in the twentieth century

A GRAMMATICAL MODEL OF A LANGUAGE is an attempt to represent systematically and overtly what the native speaker of that language intuitively knows. A model is thus a system of rules that relates patterned sounds to predictable meanings and which reflects a speaker's ability to 'make infinite use of finite means'.

As yet, there is no model for English which totally satisfies all requirements for an adequate grammar of the language, although many models have been advanced and they all have their uses. We shall look briefly at the different models advanced in this century in Britain and in the United States and we shall indicate their respective strengths and weaknesses.

Traditional Latin-influenced models

Until the 1920s, most models of English were based on Latin, the grammar of which was itself based on Greek. Study of the nature and structure of language goes back at least as far as Plato and Aristotle for western European languages. Greek was comprehensively described by Dionysius Thrax towards the end of the second century BC. All Greek words were classified in terms of case, gender, number, tense, voice and mood. Three centuries later, Apollonius Dyscolus improved on the Thrax model by including rules for combining words into acceptable sentences.

Latin grammarians adopted the Greek model for their own language and, since Greek and Latin were structurally very similar, the belief grew that grammatical categories which were valid for Greek and Latin were valid for all languages. Vernacular grammars in Europe appeared as early as the seventh century (the first was a grammar of Irish) but since Latin was the language of religion and scholarship, English and other European languages were described according to Latin categories. Where they failed to match the Latinate system they were regarded as 'debased' or 'deficient' and, if it were possible, they were modified to resemble the Latin model. This model was particularly unsuited to modern English, which is virtually an uninflected language. Let us illustrate what we mean. In Latin, a noun like 'dominus' meaning 'lord' could be declined as follows:

	singular	*plural*
nominative	dominus	domini
vocative	domine	domini
accusative	dominum	dominos
genitive	domini	dominorum
dative	domino	dominis
ablative	domino	dominis

Although Latin described six cases in the noun in both the singular and the plural, there are only eight distinct forms of 'dominus', the dative and ablative being the same and the genitive singular being identical in form to the nominative and vocative plural. Grammarians who followed the Latin model for English often declined English nouns as follows:

	singular	*plural*
nominative	lord	lords
vocative	O lord	O lords
accusative	lord	lords
genitive	lord's	lords'
dative	to the lord	to the lords
ablative	by/with/from the lord	by/with/from the lords

Notice, however, that there are only two distinct forms of 'lord', that is 'lord' and 'lords'. All the other distinctions are carried by prepositions, by an exclamatory 'O' or by the positioning of an apostrophe. If we pronounce the genitive singular, we will notice that it is identical in sound to the nominative plural, a feature that is shared by many Indo-European languages. The English verb system was even more distinct from Latin. If we consider only the simple present of 'portare' the equivalent of 'carry', we find that it is marked for person and number:

1st sing.	porto	I carry
2nd sing.	portas	you (*sing.*) carry
3rd sing.	portat	he/she/it carries
1st pl.	portamus	we carry
2nd pl.	portatis	you (*pl.*) carry
3rd pl.	portant	they carry

The equivalent English system has only two distinct forms, namely 'carry' and 'carries' but marks the gender of the subject (as being masculine, feminine or neuter) in the third person singular.

Much of the prescriptivism of school grammars derives from Latin models. Stylists have argued that English sentences should not end with a preposition because prepositions could never occur at the end of a sentence in Latin. Such a claim overlooks the fact that, in Latin, a preposition always governed a noun or pronoun and therefore could not occur without a following nominal. English, however, has always permitted prepositions to occur in sentence-final position, especially in colloquial speech. Similarly, generations of students of English have been taught that such sentences as:

It's me.

She's taller than me.

are wrong: Latin had the same case before and after the verb BE and so should English. This view, which tries to push English into a Latin mould, ignores the parallelism of such sets as:

He arrived before I did.   He's taller than I am.

He arrived before me.   He's taller than me.

It also ignores the fact that, in English, 'me' is not only accusative. It is also the emphatic form of the pronoun:

Who's there?   *Me.*

Latin-oriented grammars failed because they did not recognise that each language is unique in its organisation and patterns. Their strength lay in the fact that they recognised that languages were complex and flexible and that, at some level, languages were fundamentally similar.

Structuralism

This approach to languages developed in the US and illustrates the point that the development of any discipline is influenced by the cultural and political setting in which it evolves. In the early part of this century, grammars of languages produced in the US often differed considerably from those produced in Britain. The anthropological approach with its emphasis on the spoken medium was favoured in the US because of the existence of numerous unwritten and dying Amerindian languages. Linguists who worked on such languages carried over the skills and insights they acquired into their examination of English. In Britain, on the other hand, linguists spent a lot of time on Indic languages, many of which had long traditions of literacy and scholarship. British linguists, not unnaturally, paid more attention to the written medium and to orthographic systems.

Structuralism had one of its clearest statements in Leonard Bloomfield's *Language*, published in 1933. This model of grammar is still influential and worthy of detailed comment. Structuralists began with the premise that each language was unique and must be described in terms of its own individual patterning. They rejected such meaning-based definitions as 'a sentence is a group of words which expresses a complete idea', asking quite legitimately what an incomplete idea was, and they attempted to look on language study as a science where scientific precision would be required in all formulations.

Structuralists envisaged language as a highly structured, predictable system where one could move from sound to sentence, discovering the significant units at each level and providing rules for combining them. They started with sound and defined a 'phoneme' as the smallest unit of a language's sound system. Each language had an inventory of sounds and a linguist's task was to establish which phonemes were significant in the language being described. One step above phonemes came 'morphemes'. These were composed of phonemes and were defined as the smallest unit of syntax. There were two kinds of morphemes, bound morphemes like 'un-' which could not occur in isolation and free morphemes like 'kind' which could. Free morphemes were equivalent to words. Word classes were determined by both form and function. Nouns, for example, differed in form between singular and plural, with plurality being indicated by means of adding /s/, /z/ or /ɪz/ to the singular, thus:

gnat + /s/	>	gnats
tree + /z/	>	trees
horse + /ɪz/	>	horses

Nouns also fitted into such test frames as:

$$
\text{(the)} \ldots \ldots \text{seemed very}
\begin{cases}
\text{funny} \\
\text{good} \\
\text{happy} \\
\text{tired} \\
\text{unreliable}
\end{cases}
$$

By means of examining forms and functions of words and by means of creating test frames, structuralists avoided relying on 'meaning' and they showed that English consisted of words belonging to open classes and to closed sets. *Open classes* were groups of words like nouns, verbs, adjectives and adverbs which were potentially open-ended, that is, it would be almost impossible to list all the nouns or verbs in English largely because new ones can be created and, in addition, words can move from one class to another. ('Motown', for example, was created by blending 'motor' and 'town'. 'Motor' was originally a noun but can also be used as a verb.) *Closed sets* were words like determiners and pronouns where the items in the sets could be exhaustively listed. Among the closed sets were auxiliary verbs and prepositions which were also described as 'function words' because their primary role was to express grammatical relationships. In the sentence:

Do you like cheese?

for example, the 'do' is there to form a question but has little semantic value.

By means of such study, structuralists worked out that English contained the following word classes:

nouns

verbs (headverbs and auxiliaries)

adjectives

adverbs

determiners

prepositions

conjunctions (co-ordinating and subordinating)

pronouns

exclamations

This classification did not differ radically from the Latin-oriented model for English. Nor is this surprising in view of the fact that Latin and English are related languages. Where the structuralists did differ fundamentally from earlier linguists was: in giving priority to speech; in assuming that if native speakers used a structure regularly then that structure was correct; in ruling out reliance on meaning; in offering precise instructions for building phonemes into morphemes, morphemes into words, words into phrases, clauses and sentences; and in aiming to rely on verifiable, repeatable data.

Structuralists attempted to make the study of language as scientific as the study of chemistry. Their achievements were considerable and all subsequent models of English have utilised the discoveries and techniques of structuralism. They had weaknesses, however. Because they believed that all languages could be analysed in terms of elements in sequence, with successive elements being increasingly predictable, they undervalued the creativity of speakers and the fact that sentences could look alike and yet be very different. Such sentences as:

John asked me what to do.

and:

John persuaded me what to do.

look alike and were analysed identically by structuralists. In the first sentence, however, John was to perform the action whereas 'I' was to perform it in the second. Their techniques worked beautifully for the regular parts of English:

cat	cat+s		
mat	mat+s		
love	love+d	lov+ing	love+s
shove	shove+d	shov+ing	shove+s

but were less satisfactory for the irregular parts:

foot	foot + plural	= feet	(and not 'foots')
man	man + plural	= men	
drive	drove	driving	drives driven
sing	sang	singing	sings sung

With all their evident strengths, structuralists concentrated on the surface of the language and were more interested in analysing data than in evaluating their discoveries.

Scale and category

This model of grammar is also referred to as 'systemic' grammar and it evolved mainly due to the work of the British linguist Michael Halliday. In its earliest draft (1961), scale and category dealt only with surface structure although later modified models were aware of both surface and underlying (or deep) levels of language. This model of English is based on the existence of choice within language. The essential idea is that at any given place in a structure the language permits choice, a choice that may be extremely large or quite limited:

He	saw	his	friend	on	Monday
She	met	that	person	last	Tuesday
They	greeted	the	workman	on	Sunday
John	noticed	an	intruder	on	Friday

Even when we select such a simple sentence as 'He saw his friend on Monday' we can easily show that choice is available at every point in the sentence. It is most restricted with regard to 'on' and 'Monday' in that only 'on' and 'last' fit into the preposition slot and there are only seven weekdays. Generalising, we can show the choice by such a formula as:

Nominal + V_{past} + determiner + nominal + on/last + Xday

Scale and category grammar attempts to describe language, whether written or spoken, in terms of three primary levels:

substance ⟺ form ⟺ situation

Substance relates to sounds for the spoken medium (phonic substance) and to marks on paper for the written (graphic substance). Form is subdivided into two levels:

$$\text{form} \begin{cases} \text{lexis} \\ \text{grammar} \end{cases}$$

Lexis deals with the study of words, their shape and their ability to collocate with others. Grammar deals with the elements of a structure and with the relationships between elements. 'The blue light' and 'the light blue', for example, are both phrases but in the first phrase 'blue' modifies 'light'. We can show the similarities and differences in their structures as follows:

$_m$the $_m$blue $_h$light

$_m$the $_m$light $_h$blue

where the 'm' indicates that the words are in a subordinate or modifying role and the 'h' indicates the headword or word of prime significance in the phrase.

Situation takes into account such extralinguistic phenomena as gesture, non-linguistic noises, number of participants, time and place of occurrence. In other words, this level relates to J. R. Firth's idea of 'context of situation' which implied that an utterance could only be satisfactorily explained if the context in which it occurred was known. Let us take as an example the sentence:

That'll do.

If this is said to a child, it is usually a reprimand and it is uttered with a particular intonation pattern. If, however, it is said to a shop assistant, it implies satisfaction on the part of the client. Meaning can thus be seen to depend not only on sounds, words and structures but on context as well.

In this model, phonology was seen as linking substance and form and four units of phonology were described for English, the phoneme (or smallest significant sound unit in English), the syllable (the sound or combination of sounds marked by one element of sound prominence), the foot (which marked stress patterns in a sequence of syllables) and tone (the intonation patterns in an utterance). The five grammatical units were morpheme, word, phrase, clause and sentence and these were ranked from the smallest, 'morpheme', to the largest, 'sentence'. Sentences were described according to the categories S P O C A (Subject, Predicate, Object, Complement, Adjunct) and when the basic elements of the sentence had been described the aim was to establish systems which accounted for their form and their possible occurrence. This was done by setting up mutually exclusive features such as:

$$\text{verb phrase (VP)} \begin{cases} \text{past} \\ \text{non-past} \end{cases}$$

which indicates that a choice has to be made between the selection of the past and non-past tense in English. A more elaborate system would take other factors such as negation and finiteness into account as follows:

$$\text{VP} \begin{cases} \begin{cases} \text{negative} \\ \text{positive} \end{cases} \\ \begin{cases} \text{finite} \begin{cases} \text{past} \\ \text{non-past} \end{cases} \\ \text{non-finite} \end{cases} \end{cases}$$

The above is a very simple system network but it indicates one of the principal techniques of scale and category (systemic) grammar, which attempted to offer networks which would make explicit the relationships between all elements in a sentence.

This model was an advance on structuralism in that it tried to take into account the facts that language varies with situation and that choice is available at all levels of the language. (Later models have refined the definitions and have taken into account the creative ability of all native speakers.) Its main weakness was that it suggested that all sections of a language could be explained in terms of superficial binary contrasts.

Transformational generative grammar

In 1957 Noam Chomsky, an American, published *Syntactic Structures*, a statement of the principles of transformational generative grammar (TG). This grammar has had a profound effect on the study of all languages, including English. TG was a reaction against structuralism and the first model to acknowledge formally the significance of deep structure. We can only offer a very brief survey of the aims and characteristics of TG.

Transformational generative grammarians set themselves the task of creating an explicit model of what an ideal speaker of the language intuitively knows. Their model must assign a structure, therefore, to all the sentences of the language concerned and only to these sentences. As a first step towards this, Chomsky distinguished between 'competence', which he defines as 'the ideal speaker-hearer's knowledge of his language', and 'performance', which is 'the actual use of language in concrete situations'. Competence is, as it were, the perfect storehouse of linguistic knowledge. Performance draws on this knowledge but it can be faulty. The TG model attempts to formulate hypotheses about competence by idealising performance, that is, by dredging away performance accidents such as hesitations, unnecessary repetition, lack of attention, fatigue, slips of the tongue, false starts. TG is interested in competence and this interest marks the clearest difference between structuralism and TG. Structuralism was text-based and only interested in language that had actually occurred. TG does not use text since it is more interested in what produced the text than in the text itself.

A TG model has four main characteristics:

(1) It must attempt to make explicit how a finite entity like the brain can operate on a finite set of items (words and structures) and yet generate an infinite set of sentences. The model must parallel the ideal speaker's competence and so it must be capable of generating an infinite set of sentences by the operation of a finite set of rules on a finite set of items. We can give an impression here of how that can be done. Let us suppose, for example, that we have the rules:

S → NP + VP (sentence can be rewritten as noun phrase + verb phrase)

NP → (det) + N (noun phrase can be rewritten as (determiner) + noun)

VP → V + NP (verb phrase can be rewritten as verb + noun phrase)

and suppose we have two nouns 'boys' and 'girls', three determiners 'the', 'some' and 'five', and three verbs 'love', 'hate' and 'trust', then we can produce hundreds of sentences such as:

Boys love/hate/trust girls. ⎫
Girls love/hate/trust boys. ⎬ (6)

Some boys love/hate/trust girls.

Boys love/hate/trust some girls.

Five boys love/hate/trust the girls.

The boys love/hate/trust some/five/the girls.

These sentences give a limited idea of the productive quality of even the simplest model.

(2) Since the model attempts to describe the ideal speaker-hearer's linguistic knowledge and intuitions, it must be explicit. It must not fall back on intuition to ask whether a structure is or is not correct. If it used intuition to define intuition, the model would be circular and useless. A TG model must therefore be explicit and self-sufficient. Its rules alone must allow us to decide whether a structure is acceptable.

(3) The model must have three components: a *phonological* component, a *syntactic* component and a *semantic* component so that it parallels the speaker's ability to associate noise and meaning.

(4) Although the model must not rely on the intuition of a native speaker it must be in harmony with such intuition. In other words, it must be able to assign a structure to all sentences which would be accepted by a native speaker and reject all sentences which would be rejected by a native speaker.

The phonological component deals with phonemes and with the permissible combination of phonemes. As far as English is concerned, it offers rules for stress and intonation patterns as well. The work on phonology is an extension of the work done by structuralists, a refinement rather than a reappraisal, and this is the part of the TG model which has received least criticism. The semantic component deals with meaning and the interpretation of meaning. Much work has been done in this area and many have criticised Chomsky's techniques. It would be true to say, however, that less satisfactory work has been done with regard to semantics than with regard to phonology and syntax.

It is with regard to his treatment of syntax that Chomsky's approach differs most fundamentally from other models. TG is explicit about the fact that native speakers recognise two levels of structure. A speaker realises that:

John is easy to please

John is eager to please

may look alike but are different at some level in that the first implies:

Someone pleases John

and the second:

John pleases someone

Similarly, a native speaker recognises that although:

John loves Mary

looks very different from:

Mary is loved by John

they are fundamentally very similar. To account for the two levels that a speaker intuitively recognises, a TG model splits the syntactic component into two parts: a base subcomponent and a transformational subcomponent. The base subcomponent generates (that is, assigns a structure to) the deep underlying pattern so that we can represent it by means of a tree diagram (also called a 'labelled bracketing' and a 'phrase marker'), thus:

S → NP + VP

NP → det + N

VP → V + NP

The transformational subcomponent works on a phrase marker and so generates a surface structure. Again, a brief example may help. The structure:

det + N + V + det + N

underlies thousands of transitive sentences such as:

The cat swallowed the mouse.

The transformational subcomponent accounts for the transformation of such a sentence into such variants as:

The mouse was swallowed by the cat.

The mouse was swallowed.

The swallowing of the mouse (by the cat)

and:

The cat's swallowing of the mouse.

Transformation rules allow the grammarian to explain:

(1) deletion, for example A + B + C ⇒ A + B:

John ran away and Mary ran away ⇒ John and Mary ran away

(2) addition/insertion, for example, A + B ⇒ A + B + C:

Go away ⇒ You go away

He has come ⇒ He has just come

(3) permutation, for example, A + B + C ⇒ A + C + B:

Call John up ⇒ Call up John

(4) substitution, for example, A + B + C ⇒ A + D + C:

John arrived and Peter went in ⇒ On John's arrival Peter went in

In brief then, a TG grammar aims to pair a given string of noises with a given meaning by means of a syntactic component. The following diagram indicates how this may be done and stresses that a TG model is neutral with regard to production and reception. The arrows work both ways because a speaker can associate meaning with noise or noise with meaning:

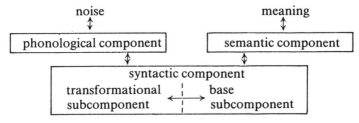

The ultimate aim of TG is the understanding of language, of the universals common to all languages, and through this an understanding of the human mind.

Case grammar

One of the values of TG is the number of sub-theories which it stimulated. Among the most interesting of these is C. J. Fillmore's case grammar (see Bibliography). Fillmore drew attention to the fact that with many verbs of change (for instance, OPEN, BREAK) essentially the same meaning could be expressed in surface structure with different nouns filling the subject slot as in:

John opened the door with a key.

The key opened the door.

The door opened.

It seems clear that, at some level, these three nouns *John, key* and *door* had a specified relationship with OPEN. Fillmore suggested that in deep structure nouns are involved in a 'case' relationship with verbs. In some languages, like Latin, the relationships show up in surface structure as case endings, whereas in English they may be indicated by sentence position and the use of prepositions. According to Fillmore, case is universal in languages and the following eight cases are sufficient to account for the relationships between verbs and nouns.

(1) **Agentive**: this case relates to the agent in a sentence, that is, to the animate instigator of the action or state identified by the verb:

Mary made a dress.

The dress was made by Mary.

Mary was a dressmaker.

The dressmaker was Mary.

'Mary' is the deep structure agent in all of the above sentences, irrespective of its surface role or position.

(2) **Experiencer**: this case relates to the animate being which is affected by the action or state identified by the verb:

John was warmed by the fire.

I threw the dog a bone.

The child believed in Santa Claus.

It infuriated John.

The underlined items above all 'experience' the activity of the verb.

(3) **Instrumental**: this is the case of the inanimate force, object or cause which is involved in the action or state identified by the verb. Again, these are underlined in the following examples:

Mary measured the curtains with a ruler.

The ruler measured the curtains.

The stone broke the window.

The curtains darkened the room.

(4) **Objective**: this case is what Fillmore refers to as his 'waste basket'. It is the case which applies to items which are contained:

John filled his pipe with tobacco.

which move or undergo change or which are affected by the action or state identified by the verb:

Smoke filled the air.

John saw the intruder.

He hit him with a stick.

He died instantly from the blow.

(5) **Source**: this is the case which marks the origin or starting point of the action or state identified by the verb:

He drove from Leeds to London.

She worked from morning until night.

The trouble began with a misunderstanding.

A misunderstanding caused the trouble.

(6) **Goal**: this marks the case of the end point or objective of the action or state identified by the verb:

He drove from London to Leeds.

He worked from morning until night.

He painted a picture.

She wrote a song.

(7) **Locative**: this case specifies the spatial orientation of the action or state identified by the verb:

The rain in Spain stays mainly on the plain.

The case was filled with books.

The flat was very comfortable.

(8) **Temporal**: this case identifies the time of the state or action identified by the verb:

Lectures end on Thursday.

We expected sunshine in the summer.

July is a pleasant month.

He arrived at noon.

Subsequent case models have varied the number of cases and aimed at greater precision but the above eight cases illustrate the techniques of case grammar. As far as English is concerned, it is necessary to fill the subject slot in all sentences except imperatives. This fact accounts for the use of dummy subjects in such sentences as:

It's raining.

where 'it' does not, in fact, refer to anything. In English, the subject slot can be filled by all the above cases:

Mary broke the cup. (Mary = agent)

John felt the pain. (John = experiencer)

The key opened the door. (key = instrument)

The cup was broken. (cup = object)

That song started the trouble. (song = source)

London was his destination. (London = goal)

It's pleasant in Greece. (Greece = location)

Spring is the loveliest time. (spring = temporal)

The attraction of Fillmore's theory is that it applies to all languages. Every group of people expresses views regarding agents and experiencers; certain actions can only be performed with an instrument; when we plant seeds we expect to have a harvest, so we all understand sources and goals; and time and place are universal realities. In Fillmore's view each deep structure sentence involves a predicator and a number of cases:

$$S \rightarrow Predicator + Case_1 + Case_2 \ldots Case_n$$

and these case markings can differ in surface structure from language to language.

The weakness of this theory is that we really do not know much about 'deep' structure, about how it is constructed or even how far below the surface of language or languages we can probe. At the deepest level of all we are trying to probe the ways the mind works and, fascinating as that study is, it is only in its infancy.

Summary

We have offered a very superficial account of five influential models of grammar. There are many others because as the flaws in one model become apparent, modified versions or new models are suggested. As we look back over the last eighty years we can see that each new model is a reaction against the perceived weaknesses of the prevailing traditions. Latin-oriented grammars lost favour because they failed to recognise the uniqueness of each language; structuralism was pushed aside because it concentrated too much on data and failed to proceed from the known to the unknown because it feared theoretical intangibles; TG and case models recognised the value of theory and the significance of what was going on beneath the surface. Their weakness is in not paying sufficient attention to surface structure where differences in form and content are most immediately apparent. Scale and category/systemic grammar has learnt much from both structuralism and TG but its potential has not yet been fully exploited. All the above models and all the others that we have not examined have strengths as well as weaknesses. The answer to an obvious question – Which model is best suited to a study of contemporary English? – can only be answered when we have the answer to another question: For what purpose do we want the model? If a model is needed for teaching English to literate adults then there is much to be said for a Latinate model; if we want a model based on language which has actually occurred and which will be useful in everyday interaction, then structuralism is still unequalled. If however, we wish to go beyond the surface of language and if we wish to explore how surface structures are related then we should turn to the more recent models.

Two facts should be apparent from our study of models: one is that we have no totally adequate model of any language in the world. A language, as we have seen, is an abstraction based on the linguistic behaviour of people. As people change and circumstances change so the language will change. Linguists are thus trying to examine a phenomenon which is never static as long as it continues to be used by people. The second fact is that we need models for different purposes and our choice of a model or a synthesis of several models will be conditioned by our needs.

Chapter 9

Branches of
linguistics

The study of language

Linguists are interested in all the languages of the world and in all the varieties that are found, the standard and the non-standard, the prestigious and the stigmatised. They recognise that languages cannot exist in any full sense without people and they are fully aware that, as a discipline, linguistics is still in its infancy. We can ask a lot of the right questions but we cannot always provide full or acceptable answers. Among the questions raised by linguists are: How did language arise? How do children acquire it? Why does it change? Are all human languages related? How can we teach and learn languages that are not our mother tongues? Why do people in all countries and in all conditions have both a language and a literature? We shall start with the first question and then indicate how linguistics has subdivided in the attempt to study aspects of language more closely and more systematically.

The simplest answer to the question: How did language arise? is that we do not know. Nor is it likely that we shall ever know. It has been suggested that our ancestors left the forests for the plains hundreds of thousands of years ago and that their new conditions demanded a much more complex signalling system. Gradually, it is argued, human beings began to use a system of sounds that was not limited by time or in space. By this we mean that human beings would not only make noises in the presence of danger, but learned to relate experiences and even to anticipate them verbally. It is possible that human languages evolved from primitive signalling systems – possible but not provable.

First, our records of language use go back less than six thousand years and these records reveal languages that were just as complex, just as precise, as their modern counterparts. Secondly, all modern languages studied are equally capable of expressing the linguistic needs of their users. People may live in primitive conditions but this does not mean that their languages are simple or lacking in subtlety. As George Steiner (see Bibliography) graphically puts it: 'starving bands of Amazonian Indians may lavish on their condition more verb tenses than could Plato' (*After Babel*, p. 55). Thirdly, although linguists have studied language for at least three thousand years, we have no comprehensive or totally satisfactory grammar of any living language. And yet children learn the language or languages of their environment easily and completely and, it must be added, without any obvious instruction. Perhaps the best we can do is study today's languages and when our knowledge is more complete we may then be able to offer more comprehensive theories for the origin of language. They will be theories, however, and not answers.

Sociolinguistics

This branch of linguistics concentrates on language in society, in other words, it tries to examine how and why people use language as they interact with other members of their society. Sociolinguistics examines variety in language and has shown that language is not merely used to communicate ideas but also to communicate our opinion of others and of ourselves. Even the simplest utterance such as 'Hello!' can reveal that the speaker wishes to be friendly and informal, and that he or she is probably British (many Americans would prefer 'Hi!'). In considering any spoken communication, therefore, a student will notice that a speaker's language reveals information on his sex, approximate age, regional and perhaps ethnic origins, education and attitude to his listeners. Variation also occurs in terms of the subject matter under discussion: nuclear disarmament will not be discussed in the same terms as neighbourly gossip. Nor will one use identical forms of language with a shopkeeper and a minister of religion. Speakers can also range in formality from the shared intimacy of slang through casual conversation to the stiff correctness that usually characterises an interview. Variety, then, and not unchanging monotony is the norm in mother-tongue usage and so sociolinguistics studies how, when, why and in what ways variation occurs.

Not all communities are monolingual and so linguists have examined language use in bilingual and multilingual communities too. In such communities, one language may signal a degree of education and another may indicate friendliness. The Belgian who switches from French to Flemish is not just showing that he has mastered two languages. He may be indicating his opinion of the listener, suggesting, for example, that he recognises the listener as one who shares his cultural background.

In multilingual communities, lingua francas have often grown up as a means of permitting communication where previously little or none existed. Interestingly, where such lingua francas have developed, whether in Africa, America, Asia, Australia or Europe, they show remarkable similarities. Initially this similarity surprised linguists but the greater our knowledge grows, the more we realise that human beings are similar and human needs are similar, so perhaps it would be even more surprising if our techniques for communicating proved to be very different.

Sociolinguists thus set themselves the tasks of examining language use, its variation, its development, change and standardisation, its regional and class dialects, its lingua francas, its specialised codes. Much has been learnt, including the fact that we use language as often to exclude others as we do to establish bonds. The greater our knowledge grows, however, the more we are forced to recognise the extraordinary flexibility and complexity of all human systems of communication.

Psycholinguistics

This branch deals with the relationship between language and the mind, focusing mainly on how language is learnt, stored and occasionally lost. The relationship between language and mind has two aspects, acquisition and performance, and the two are intimately linked. What we acquire is the ability to perform, that is, to use language with appropriateness, and performance is essential to complete and successful acquisition. Knowledge of this interlocking relationship underlies most successful language teaching and so we shall return to it in our section on applied linguistics.

The basic fact calling for explanation in this area is the remarkably short time that a child takes to acquire an extensive knowledge of, and high degree of control over, the language or languages of his environment. Expressing this another way, we can say that a normal child of five has, without any obvious difficulty, learnt to control a language that no mature linguist can fully explain. Let us look a little closer at what a child of five can actually do: he can understand utterances that he has never heard before; produce sentences that are totally new to him and to his listeners; and he can use his knowledge of speech to acquire the new skills of writing and reading. He can do all of this because, somehow, he has managed to extract from the speech he has heard the underlying system of the language. Furthermore, he has acquired essentially the same underlying system as all his little friends, in spite of the fact that no two children are exposed to identical circumstances or to the same samples of language.

During the past forty years there have been two main theories to account for the phenomenon of language learning by children. The first, known as 'behaviourism', was fully formulated by B. F. Skinner in *Verbal Behaviour* (1957). This theory claims that language learning in children can be accounted for in very much the same way as we can account for a dog learning to stand on its hind legs to beg for a biscuit: training, stimulation, imitation, reward and repetition.

The second theory, known as 'mentalism', argues that just as human children are genetically programmed to walk when they reach a certain stage of development, so they are programmed to talk. Research suggests that all children of all nationalities, irrespective of race, class or intelligence, learn language in regular steps, moving from babbling to one-word utterances, then to combining two words until their speech is indistinguishable from the adult norms of their community. Mentalists suggest that language is as natural a part in the development of human beings as the growth of the body. Given the right environment, that is, exposure to speech, a child automatically acquires language. Obviously, if a child is not exposed to language he will not learn it. Perhaps an analogy will help here. A child is not a miniature speaker but a potential one in the same way as an acorn is not a miniature oak tree, but, given the right environment, it will become an oak.

Psycholinguists also attempt to understand dysphasia (literally 'bad speech'), dyslexia (word blindness) and aphasia (the sudden or gradual loss of language due to age, an accident or a stroke). We all have experience of aphasia when we cannot remember the word for something or when we say: 'Put that in the fridge' when we mean the oven or the cupboard. Such slips are commonplace and are made by all users of language when they are tired or tense or getting old. The slips we make are extremely interesting. Notice, for example, that the items 'fridge', 'oven' and 'cupboard' have a great deal in common. They are all nouns, all receptacles for food, all in the kitchen and all with large doors. Such slips suggest that we may store words with similar meanings together. Other slips such as using a word like 'woollen' when we mean 'wooden' suggest that we may store some words, especially adjectives, according to sound.

Psycholinguists have learnt a great deal and are daily learning more about how we use, abuse and lose language. They too have discovered the non-finite nature of language. Some problems have been solved. (Deaf children can be helped to better enunciation if they are fitted with a hearing device shortly after birth.) But each solution has revealed how little we really know about language and how much more research is needed.

Applied linguistics

Travellers have always known that communication depends on the ability to modify language use. Sometimes the modifications required are relatively slight, as when a Londoner wants to get directions from a

Scot. Often, they are much greater and involve the use of a language other than one's mother tongue. People have been learning other languages throughout recorded history and two facts seem to have been known always:
(1) that any human language is capable of being translated into any other and
(2) that word-for-word translation is inadequate. To have a good knowledge of another language means acquiring something of the native speaker's innate knowledge.

Recently, the insights gained in sociolinguistics and psycholinguistics have been applied to language teaching and learning. Courses in English for Special Purposes (ESP) are based on the knowledge that native speakers use language differently depending on subject matter and audience, for example. Therefore, a scientist who needs English will not need to know how to discuss Dickens or diplomacy but will have to learn all the technical terms associated with his profession and the preferred structures that scientists use. Scientists use more passive structures when they write than non-scientists do. It is clearly useful, therefore, to teach passives to scientists who need to learn some English.

Insights from psycholinguistics have resulted in foreign languages being taught to children earlier since we seem to lose our linguistic flexibility at puberty. They have also led to an awareness that the errors made by learners can be useful in suggesting the hypotheses learners make as they master their target language.

Many techniques have evolved for the efficient teaching of languages, techniques involving contrastive analysis (a detailed examination of both mother tongue and target language and the pinpointing of potential areas of difficulty) and error analysis. Others have concentrated on the learner, examining the way he creates successive 'interlanguages' as he moves from modelling the target language on his mother tongue to a fuller control of the target.

It is certainly true that language laboratories and modified teaching strategies have resulted in a better grasp of the spoken medium and in a quicker grasp of the basic tools necessary to permit elementary communication. It is, however, doubtful that any one technique will ever become a linguistic philosopher's stone capable of transforming hesitant learners into fluent speakers. Used by a good teacher any method can produce students who master the intricacies of a foreign language. And no method, however linguistically sanctioned, will work without motivation, practice, reinforcement and, most of all, the opportunity to use the acquired language for tasks for which it would be used by the native speaker.

Stylistics

Few linguists would deny that literature is 'language at full stretch' and therefore less easy to describe and explain than a conversation in the street. Most would also admit that a purely linguistic analysis will never explain why we can be moved by a particular pattern of words – why, for example, we may have little or no reaction to: 'I wish that person were still alive!' and be strongly affected by Tennyson's:

> But O for the touch of a vanished hand,
> And the sound of a voice that is still!

Yet all linguists would claim that literature, whether written or oral, is composed of language and so is amenable to linguistic analysis. Some would even argue that a work which is diminished by a detailed study of its form was not great literature in the first place.

Literary stylistics is the area of study where the linguist combines with the critic so as to achieve a fuller understanding and appreciation of literature, and studies have shown that a knowledge of phonology, morphology, vocabulary, syntax, rhetorical and graphological devices can help to make overt what the sensitive reader of literature has always been covertly aware of. Let us look briefly at some of the literary insights gained from linguistics.

Phonology has shown us how individual sounds are made and helps explain why plosives which are sharp, staccato sounds, are often used to recreate the sounds of modern warfare; and why fricatives like 's' and 'z' are used to emphasise continuous and perhaps sinuous movements. Morphology studies word formation and the art of what is possible in language. Literature often goes beyond the possible, permitting Larry Burns's play with morphemes:

> In my dotage I've become
> Inert, defunct, inane.
> Oh, to be like yester-year,
> Ert, funct and ane again.

and the experimentation of Gerard Manley Hopkins's:

> I caught this morning morning's minion, king-
> dom of daylight's dauphin, dapple-dawn-drawn Falcon, in his
> [riding

Graphology (the study of conventions in writing and printing) has made us aware of the difficulties faced by a writer who wishes his heroine to speak a rural dialect. If he offers a true representation of dialectal speech he runs the risk of making his heroine appear either funny or stupid or both. Writers therefore use dialectal markings very sparingly in the recreation of non-standard speech.

Stylistics thus exploits our knowledge of linguistic variety, our awareness of the appropriateness of certain combinations and provides us with the tools necessary to deepen our awareness of literature. It is not, however, an alternative to sensitive intuition, but a means of exploring and reinforcing such intuition.

Summary

As we learn language, we learn to classify. We learn that apples and oranges are fruit and that milk and water are drinks. In linguistics, we use language to classify language and this is by no means an easy task. However scientific we may try to be, we carry to our study many of the experiences and attitudes we absorbed as we acquired our mother tongue. Because of this we can never be as objective about language as we can be about the objects we classify by means of language. Strides have been made in understanding parts of the linguistic jigsaw but so far we have either not collected all the necessary pieces or have not yet learnt how to fit them together so that the complete story of language emerges.

Answers to exercises

Chapter 2

1. (a) bilabial
   (b) labiodental
   (c) alveolar
   (d) palatal
   (e) velar

2. (a) affricate
   (b) nasal
   (c) lateral
   (d) fricative
   (e) plosive

3. (a) b   boat
   (b) m   mat
   (c) f   fat
   (d) l   let
   (e) i   see
   (f) u   room
   (g) z   zoo
   (h) r   rat
   (i) k   call
   (j) ð   that

4. (a) b – all the others are nasals
   (b) n – „ „ „   „   plosives
   (c) s – „ „ „   „   bilabials
   (d) l – „ „ „   „   fricatives
   (e) l – „ „ „   „   vowels
   (f) o – „ „ „   „   front vowels
   (g) p – „ „ „   „   alveolars
   (h) d – „ „ „   „   voiceless
   (i) s – „ „ „   „   voiced
   (j) t – „ „ „   „   velars

5. (a) f is a voiceless labiodental fricative; v is a voiced labiodental
       fricative
   (b) ss   represents /ʃ/   which is a voiceless palato-alveolar fricative
       z   „   /ʒ/   which is a voiced palato-alveolar fricative

(c) *d* is a voiced alveolar plosive; *t* is a voiceless alveolar plosive

(d) *ea* represents /i/   which is a front close unrounded vowel

    e   "   /ɛ/   "   "   front half-open unrounded vowel

(e) *j*   "   /dʒ/   "   "   voiced palato-aveolar fricative

   sh   "   /ʃ/   "   "   voiceless palato-alveolar fricative

(f) *t*   "   /ʃ/   "   "   voiceless palato-alveolar fricative

   dd   "   /d/   "   "   voiced alveolar plosive

(g) *gh*   "   /f/   "   "   voiceless labiodental fricative

   b   "   /b/   "   "   voiced bilabial plosive

(h) *ee*   "   /i/   "   "   front close unrounded vowel

   a   "   /ɔ/   "   "   back half-open rounded vowel

(i) *v*   "   /v/   "   "   voiced labiodental fricative

   w   "   /w/   "   "   bilabial semi-vowel

(j) *ng*   "   /ŋ/   "   "   velar nasal

   n   "   /n/   "   "   an alveolar nasal

Chapter 3

1. (1) pig, big
    (2) time, dime
    (3) came, game
    (4) sip, zip
    (5) share, chair
    (6) son, sung
    (7) man, pan
    (8) note, dote
    (9) rain, lane
   (10) chin, gin

2. (1) /goʊst/
    (2) /əmʌŋ/
    (3) /ɪnfɪltreit/
    (4) /famjɑd/
    (5) /tʃʌtni/
    (6) /dʒʌdʒɪŋ/
    (7) /splɛndɪd/
    (8) /ʌndəpɪnd/
    (9) /θaʊzəntθs/
   (10) /bjutɪfəl/

3. (1) short
    (2) treasure
    (3) cute
    (4) you, 'u', ewe

(5) meat, meet, mete
(6) church
(7) tongue
(8) weather, whether
(9) jazz
(10) everything

4. (1) (*a*) /bɜd/   (*b*) /bɜrd/
    (2) (*a*) /grɑs/   (*b*) /græs/
    (3) (*a*) /nju/   (*b*) /nu/
    (4) (*a*) /kɑsəl/   (*b*) /kæsəl/
    (5) (*a*) /fɑmjɑd/   (*b*) /fɒrmjɒrd/
    (6) (*a*) /brɛd/   (*b*) /brɛd/
    (7) (*a*) /fɛə/   (*b*) /fɛr/
    (8) (*a*) /stjʊəd/   (*b*) /stʊərd/
    (9) (*a*) /hɔl/   (*b*) /hɔl/
    (10) (*a*) /hoʊl/   (*b*) /hoʊl/

5. (1) 'apple
    (2) di'vision
    (3) 'duly
    (4) 'fashionable
    (5) infil'tration
    (6) lo'botomy
    (7) photo'graphic
    (8) (*n.*) 'object, (*v.*) ob'ject
    (9) uni'versity
    (10) zo'ology

Chapter 4

1. (1) equal + ise + er + s (ise+er>iser)
    (2) incline + ation (e+ation>ation)
    (3) be + friend + ing
    (4) trans + port + ation
    (5) en + dear + ment
    (6) pre + determine + ation (e+ation>ation)
    (7) danger + ous + ly
    (8) un + believe + able (e+able>able)
    (9) protect + ion
    (10) de + human + ise*

* For students who know Latin, it is possible to break down some of the above words into smaller units, but our segmentation is sufficient for English.

2. (1) ion (D) + al (D)
   (2) ing (I)
   (3) ise (D) + ed (I) (e +ed>ed)
   (4) ise (D) + s (I)
   (5) re (D) + er (D) +s (I)
   (6) able (D) + ly (D) (able +ly>ably)
   (7) re (D) + s(I)
   (8) s (I)
   (9) pre (D) + ed (I)
   (10) sub (D) + er (D) + s (I) (ine +er>iner)

3. (1) s, z, ız – cuts, sees, dances
   (2) t, d, ıd – looked, rained, listed
   (3) il, im, in, ir – illogical, impolite, interminable, irrational

4. (1) un + *bear* + able – able changes the word class
   (2) *moral* + ise + d – ise changes the word class
   (3) *tranquil* + ise + er + s – both -ise and -er change the word class
   (4) im + *prudent* + ly – ly changes the word class
   (5) *wide* + th – th changes the word class

5. (1) non (D) – some
   (2) ese (D) – many
   (3) ation (D) – many
   (4) ing (I) + s (I) – many + many
   (5) multi (D) – few
   (6) inter (D) + al (D) – few + many
   (7) ed (I) – many
   (8) 's (I) – many
   (9) mid (D) – few
   (10) less (D) – many

Chapter 5

---

1. (1) (*a*) 5, (*b*) 5, (*c*) 2, (*d*) 5
   (2) (*a*) 5, (*b*) 5, (*c*) 3, (*d*) 5
   (3) (*a*) 5, (*b*) 5, (*c*) 2, (*d*) 5
   (4) (*a*) 3, (*b*) 1, (*c*) 3, (*d*) 3
   (5) (*a*) 3, (*b*) 3, (*c*) 3, (*d*) 1

2. (1) a yard surrounding a farm
   (2) a mouse which lives in the fields
   (3) a girl who is a friend
   (4) a house where the temperature is kept high
   (5) a house in which plays are performed

(6) a man who delivers the post/mail
(7) a coat which protects one from the rain
(8) a worm which produces silk
(9) a boat which uses steam to drive the engine
(10) a house which is built in a tree

3. (1) a ball for the feet (noun + noun)
   (2) a house for green plants (adjective + noun)
   (3) a saw that is held in the hand (noun + noun)
   (4) a life style which is very pleasurable (adjective + noun)
   (5) wool that comes from a lamb (or lambs) (noun + noun)
   (6) money that comes in (adverb + verb)
   (7) man who delivers milk (noun + noun)
   (8) what one sees looking out or into the future (adverb + verb/noun)
   (9) something to scare crows (verb + noun)
   (10) something (usually food) that people take away (verb + adverb)

4. (1) verb, adverb, pronoun
   (2) determiner, noun, adverb
   (3) auxiliary/dummy verb, relative pronoun/subordinating conjunction, verb
   (4) preposition, pronoun, pronoun
   (5) conjunction, preposition, possessive adjective
   (6) exclamation, pronoun, verb
   (7) noun, verb, noun
   (8) adverb, adjective, adverb
   (9) adverb, adjective, possessive pronoun
   (10) pronoun, modal verb/auxiliary verb, preposition

Chapter 6

1. (1) 'three boxes of biscuits': Noun Phrase; 'on the 14th of July': Prep. P.
   (2) 'All the children': Noun P.; 'extremely happy': Adj. P.
   (3) 'couldn't go': Verb P.; 'to the fête': Prep. P; 'because of her bad cold': Adv. P.
   (4) 'To have played football': Verb P.; 'for Manchester United': Prep. P.; 'his greatest achievement': Noun P.
   (5) 'will have arrived': Verb P.; 'in Spain': Prep. P.; 'by this time': Prep. P.

2. (1) that they would have enough money (object)
   (2) What we heard (subject)
   (3) what one might describe as agitated (complement)

(4) all I can remember (complement)
(5) 'Who was she?' (subject)
(NB: 'that everyone asked' is an adjective clause.)

3. (1) Main Cl. I shall always remember; Sub. Cl. what you said = Noun Cl.
(2) Main Cl. everyone was asleep; Sub. Cl. When we arrived = Adv. Cl.
(3) Main Cl. It was; Sub. Cl. what everyone had feared = Noun Cl.
(4) Main Cl. He arrived on the very day; Sub. Cl. when we were celebrating your birthday = Adj. Cl. (NB: 'when' = 'on which')
(5) Main Cl. The hat was the wrong colour; Sub. Cl. which I bought = Adj. Cl.

4. (1) (a) Come at eight o'clock. (b) Will he come at eight o'clock?
(2) (a) Don't do that. (b) Doesn't she do that?
(3) (a) Try to help. (b) Does she try to help?
(4) (a) Don't play cricket. (b) Doesn't he play cricket?
(5) (a) Be serious. (b) Can't you be serious?

5. (1) (a) minor (b) simple
(2) (a) major (b) complex
(3) (a) minor (b) simple
(4) (a) major (b) compound
(5) (a) major (b) complex
(6) (a) major (b) complex
(7) (a) major (b) simple
(8) (a) minor (b) compound
(9) (a) major (b) complex
(10) (a) minor (b) simple

Chapter 7

---

1. There are a number of possible answers in 1(1) to 1(10). We provide only one in each case.
(1) small, very small
(2) regal
(3) concealed   parents
(4) bad smell
(5) Show me the way to my home.
(6) stand   din
(7) a workman
(8) ignited
(9) dozes (off)
(10) interfere   belongings

2. There are a number of possible answers in 2(1) to 2(10). Again, we provide only one of several acceptable alternatives.
   (1) largest
   (2) hot
   (3) warm
   (4) warm
   (5) fair
   (6) bright
   (7) clear
   (8) appeared
   (9) departed
   (10) narrow

3. (1)

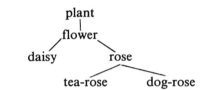

```
                plant
                  |
               flower
              /        \
          daisy          rose
                        /      \
                  tea-rose      dog-rose
```

(2)

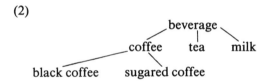

```
                   beverage
                 /     |     \
            coffee    tea     milk
           /      \
   black coffee   sugared coffee
```

(3)

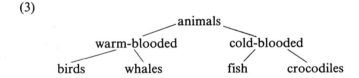

```
                    animals
                 /           \
       warm-blooded          cold-blooded
       /      \              /        \
   birds    whales       fish      crocodiles
```

4.

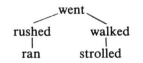

```
              went
            /      \
        rushed      walked
          |           |
         ran        strolled
```

'rushed' and 'strolled' are mutually exclusive and so are 'rushed' and 'walked', 'ran' and 'walked', and 'ran' and 'strolled'.

5. (1) as right as rain
   (2) a blue moon
   (3) by the skin of his teeth

(4) burn the candle at both ends
(5) bark up the wrong tree
(6) cry for the moon
(7) go on a wild goose chase
(8) bite the dust/the hand that feeds you/the bullet
(9) keep a low profile
(10) get to the nitty gritty

Glossary of useful terms

active voice: this term applies to a sentence or clause where the subject is the agent or the instigator of the action:

John cried.

John watched the football match.

John kicked the ball.

All sentences involving intransitive verbs are active:

John arrived.

John ran away.

Active sentences involving transitive verbs can be transformed into passives:

The football match was watched (by John).

The ball was kicked (by John).

The sentences are called truncated passives when by + agent is deleted. Active sentences have the forms:

NP + intransitive verb

NP_1 + transitive verb + NP_2

Passive sentences have the form:

NP_2 + BE + past participle of verb (by + NP_1).

adjective phrase: a constituent of a sentence, comprising a group of words which modifies a noun. It can be either attributive (usually preceding, occasionally following a noun) or predicative (following a verb).

adverb phrase: a constituent of a sentence, a group of words which functions like an adverb.

affix: a bound morpheme that can be added to the base form of a word. Affixes are of two kinds in English, prefixes which precede the base form, and suffixes which follow. If we take 'man' as our base form, we can add the prefix 'un-' and the suffix '-ly' producing 'unmanly'.

affricate: a consonant involving a closure in the mouth as for a plosive followed by a slow release of air producing friction. The initial sounds in 'chump' and 'jump' are affricates.

alliteration: the repetition of consonant sounds in adjacent syllables:

Round and round the rugged rock the ragged rascal ran.

allomorph: a conditioned form of a morpheme. The negative morpheme 'in', for example, can become 'il/im/ir' depending on the following consonant, for example, illegal, immoral, irrespective.

allophone: a conditioned variant of a phoneme. The 'l' sounds in 'light' and 'full' are allophones in English, the former sound always being used initially in words or syllables and the latter occurring in word-final position.

alveolar: a consonant formed by approximating the tip of the tongue to the ridge behind the upper teeth. In English, the initial sounds in 'tap', 'nap' and 'sap' are alveolar.

antonyms: words of approximately opposite meanings, for example 'good' and 'bad', 'young' and 'old'.

applied linguistics: application of the discoveries of linguistics to the teaching and learning of languages.

aspect: a category of the verb which concentrates attention on whether an event is completed (I have read the book), continuing (I am reading the book) or habitual (I read for an hour every morning).

assonance: the repetition of the same vowel sound in adjacent words: How now brown cow?

auxiliary verbs: verbs which help in the formation of questions, negatives, aspect, passive voice and modality. The auxiliaries in English are: BE, DO, HAVE and the modals: can, could, may, might, must, shall, should, will, would.

base form: also called the 'root' and the 'stem'. This is the unmodified form of a word. 'Child', 'see' and 'small' are base forms, 'children', 'sees' and 'smaller' are modified forms. The base form of a noun is identical with its singular: the base form of a verb is the same as the imperative.

base subcomponent: a subdivision of syntax in transformational grammar. The base contains rules which underlie sentences and which give details for specifying the vocabulary of a language.

bilabial: a consonant made by approximating the lips. In English the initial sounds in 'pat', 'bat', 'mat' are bilabial.

case grammar: a grammatical model which focuses on the deep structure relationships between a predicate and the noun phrases in a sentence. Certain relationships such as Agent, Location, Instrument are regarded as being universal in languages.

clause: a group of words larger than a phrase and smaller than a sentence and having a subject and a predicate. Clauses can be divided into:

(1) Main clauses and subordinate or dependent clauses. In a sentence like:

(I chased him) but (he got away).

we have two main clauses (clauses of equal grammatical weight and each capable of occurring alone). In:

(When I chased him) (he ran away).

we have a subordinate clause (when I chased him) and a main clause (he ran away).

(2) Finite and non-finite clauses. Non-finite clauses contain the non-finite verb forms: the infinitive (to come), the present participle (arriving) and the past participle (taken):
   'When I arrived' is a finite clause, 'On arriving' is a non-finite clause in the sentences:

When I arrived I went straight to his house.

On arriving I went straight to his house.

(3) There are three types of clauses:
   adjective/relative clauses:

The man (who wore a black hat) was my father.

adverb clauses:

I shall go (if you come with me).

and noun clauses:

(That food prices are high) is an indisputable fact.
cohesion: the means of linking sentences into larger units such as paragraphs. Cohesion may involve noun and verb substitutes, similarity of time references and, in certain circumstances, devices like rhyme, assonance and alliteration.
collocate: occur side by side.
competence: the idealised knowledge of a language possessed by an ideal speaker-hearer.
complement: unit necessary to complete a sentence. Complements can be of several types:

John is a good boy. —   noun phrase complement
John is fat.   —   adjective complement
John is out.   —   adverb complement

The above are called subject complements because they add to our knowledge of the subject. We can also have object complements:

They elected John Smith President.

He called his brother a fool.

complementarity: the relationship between pairs of words, in which the denial of one implies the assertion of the other, for instance 'male' and 'female'.

copula: verb which needs a complement. BE is the commonest copula in the language but the following verbs can also be used as copulas: APPEAR, BECOME, GROW, SEEM as in:

He was/appeared/became/grew/seemed tired.

deep structure: a notion fundamental to transformational grammar stressing the fact that native speakers recognise two levels of language: the surface structure (actual samples of spoken or written language) and a deeper structure where sentences like:

John helped Mary.

and:

Mary was helped by John.

would be shown to be similar in form as well as meaning.

dental: a consonant involving the approximation of the tip of the tongue to the upper teeth. The initial sounds in 'thin' and 'then' are dentals.

diphthong: a sound involving the movement of the tongue from one vowel position to another. The central sound in 'get' is a monophthong, involving only one vowel sound, but the central sound in 'gate' involves a movement from /e/ towards /i/.

ergative: a term meaning 'cause' applied to the relationship between such pairs of sentences as:

(*a*) The plate broke.

(*b*) John broke the plate.

where the subject of (*a*) becomes the object of the same verb and a new causative subject is introduced as in (*b*).

finite verb: a verb than can take a subject from the pronouns 'I', 'he', 'she', 'it', 'we', 'they'. Thus 'see', 'sees', 'saw', are the finite forms of SEE and 'to see', 'seeing', 'seen' the non-finite parts.

fricative: a consonant involving the restriction but not the total stoppage of the air stream. The initial sounds in 'vat' and 'sat' are fricatives.

headverb: verb which carries the information in a sentence. In a sentence such as 'He was seen', 'seen' is the headverb, 'was' is an auxiliary verb which helps to make the information carried by the headverb 'seen' more precise.

homographs: words which have the same spelling but different meanings and pronunciation, for instance, 'read' in:

Read (rhymes with 'seed') your book quietly.

I read (rhymes with 'bed') that book last year.

homonyms: words which have the same form but different meanings, for example, 'ear' (for hearing) and 'ear' (of corn).

homophones: words which sound the same but have different meanings, for example 'pair' and 'pear'; 'too' and 'two'.

hyponymy: relationship of implicit inclusion between words, for instance the word 'red' includes the colours 'scarlet' and 'vermilion'.

idiom: a group of words whose meaning cannot be deduced from the habitual meanings of the individual words. A 'hot potato', for example, is neither 'hot' nor 'a potato'.

imperative: a sentence giving a command or making a strong suggestions. Imperatives use the base form of the verb:

Come here. Please don't do it.

ingressive: (of sound) made with air sucked in through the mouth.

interrogative: a sentence which asks a question. There are two types of interrogatives in English, those requiring a 'yes' or 'no' answer such as:

Have you seen John?

and those involving question words like 'who?', 'when?', 'why?' which require a longer answer.

labiodental: a consonant formed by approximating the lower lip and the upper teeth. The initial sounds in 'fine' and 'vine' are labiodentals.

langue and parole: terms introduced by Ferdinand de Saussure and similar to the Chomskyan distinction between 'competence' and 'performance'. 'Langue' is the comprehensive language knowledge of a community; 'parole' is the individual's use of language and suffers from imperfections due to limited knowledge, fatigue, carelessness. 'Parole' is essentially the same as 'performance' but 'langue' and 'competence' differ. Both are idealisations but 'langue' is based on the total knowledge of a speech community whereas 'competence' is the language knowledge of an ideal speaker-hearer in a homogeneous speech community.

linguistics: the scientific study of language.

metaphor: a figure of speech whereby the attributes of one item are transferred to another. If we say:

My love is like a rose

we are using a simile. When we say:

My love is beautiful but has thorns.

then we are using a metaphor.

modal verbs: a set of nine auxiliaries: *can, could, may, might, must, shall, should, will, would.* These verbs are unique in the language in terms of their grammar: they come first in a verb phrase, can take 'not/n't' directly, do not show agreement with a subject. They are used to express ability, doubt, necessity, obligation, possibility and probability.

monophthong: *see* diphthong.

morpheme: the smallest unit of grammar. A bound morpheme cannot occur alone. In the word 'books' we have two morphemes, the free morpheme 'book' which can occur in isolation and the bound morpheme '-s' which indicates plurality.

negation: a system of denying or refuting a proposition. Negation is usually marked by the use of 'not/n't' or other 'n-' words such as 'neither . . . nor', 'never', 'no', 'none'. It can also be implied by the use of verbs like 'deny', 'refute' and by adverbs like 'hardly' or 'scarcely'.

noun phrase: a constituent of a sentence with a noun or noun-like word as its most significant element. This element is called the 'headword'. In the noun phrases: 'the good book' and 'my fine friend', 'book' and 'friend' are the headwords. In transformational grammar, a pronoun is regarded as a noun phrase because of its ability to replace other noun phrases.

object: a noun phrase that habitually follows the predicate. We can have both direct and indirect objects. A direct object can become the subject of a sentence when it is passivised, thus:

John planted the tree.

The tree was planted by John.

An indirect object is the person or thing for whom something is done or to whom something is given:

He built his wife a house/He built a house for his wife

'House' is the direct object in the above sentences and 'his wife' the indirect object.

parole: *see* langue and parole.

passive voice: sentences with transitive verbs can have two forms:

John ate the bananas. — active

The bananas were eaten (by John). — passive

Passive sentences allow us the choice of omitting the agent, the person or thing which performed the action.

performance: actual language data as opposed to the idealised competence which is assumed to underlie performance.

phoneme: the smallest significant unit of sound in a language. Different words can be distinguished by the use of different phonemes. In English, /p/ and /t/ are distinct phonemes and can be used to distinguish many words, for instance 'pack' and 'tack', 'pin' and 'tin', 'pop' and 'top'.

phonetics: the study of how sounds are produced and perceived. Phoneticians have created an alphabet writing system called the International Phonetics Association/IPA chart which allows all languages to be transcribed systematically.

phonology: the study of sounds and sound combinations in a particular language.

phrase: a group of words functioning as a unit. In the sentence:

The young boy will be arriving on the next train.

we have three phrases: a noun phrase 'The young boy', a predicate phrase 'will be arriving' and a preposition phrase 'on the next train'.

pitch: speech melody, the normal rise and fall of the voice in speech.

plosive: a consonant formed by a complete closure in the vocal tract followed by a sudden release of the air. The initial sounds in 'pan' and 'ban' are plosives. Plosives are sometimes referred to as 'stops'.

polysemy: this term refers to the fact that one word may have several meanings. 'Chop', for example, means both 'cut down' and 'piece of meat'. Many English words are polysemous, that is, have a range of different meanings.

predicator: traditional grammar often used the word 'verb' in two different ways: to describe a part of speech such as 'Go', 'Come', 'Move'; and to describe the verbal constituent in a sentence:

Mary (subject)   loved (verb)   cake (object)

The term 'predicate' was introduced to refer to all that follows the subject:

Subject	Predicate
John	died suddenly.
John	loved Mary.

The term 'predicator' refers specifically to the verbal part of a sentence:

Subject	Predicator	Object	Adverb
John	died		suddenly.
John	loved	Mary.	

prefix: the affix which is added to the beginning of a word. *See under* affix.

preposition phrase: a group of words in a sentence which begins with a preposition.

pronoun: a member of a finite set of units which can replace nouns and noun phrases. There are several types of pronoun: personal pronouns such as 'I', 'you', 'us', demonstrative pronouns such as 'this', 'those', interrogative pronouns such as 'who?', 'which?', and indefinite pronouns such as 'one', 'some'.

psycholinguistics: the study of the relationship between language and the mind with special attention being paid to the way language is acquired, stored and lost.

relative clauses: adjective clauses often introduced by 'that', 'who', 'whom', 'which'.

retroflex: (of a sound) made with the tip of the tongue curling towards the hard palate.

root: the base form of a word, that is, a noun that is unmarked for plurality or possession, a verb that is unmarked for tense or person an adjective or adverb which is unmarked for comparative or superlative.

semantics: the study of meaning.

simile: *see* metaphor.

sociolinguistics: the study of the ways people use language with special attention being paid to variation within a language.

structuralism: the detailed study of the forms and functions of a language based on the assumption that every language is unique and can only be studied in terms of its own individual patterning.

stylistics: the insights provided by linguistics in the study of texts, especially literary texts.

subject: the noun phrase or subject pronoun which occurs before the predicate in an affirmative sentence, within the predicate in an interrogative sentence and which causes the modification of the predicate in the non-past tense:

The man will come tomorrow.

Will the man come tomorrow?

The man always comes on a bicycle.

suffix: the affix which is added to the end of words. '-ise' is a suffix in 'hospitalise'. *See also under* affix.

suprasegmentals: features of speech which extend over more than one sound. Suprasegmental features include loudness, intonation, stress and speed of utterance.

surface structure: actual samples of language that can be heard or read. Often sentences may look alike on the surface:

(*a*) The child is too small to play football.

(*b*) The child is too small to pick up.

but be fundamentally different in meaning. Sentence (*a*) implies that the child cannot play football; (*b*) that someone else should not pick up the child.

synonyms: words of approximately the same meaning: 'Autumn' and 'Fall', 'big' and 'large', 'adore' and 'worship'.

syntax: the arrangement of words into larger units such as phrases, clauses, sentences.

tense: time markings in the verb:

He sings — non-past reference

He sang — past reference.

Time is not to be equated with tense. Often in English time is indicated by the use of adverbs:

He sings in the choir every day.

He sings in the choir tomorrow.

transformational subcomponent: a subdivision of syntax in transformational grammar. The transformation subcomponent accounts for the transformation of a sentence into variants, such as for example:

The cat swallowed a mouse.

The mouse was swallowed by the cat.

The swallowing of a mouse (by the cat).

transformational generative grammar (TG): a model of grammar which tries to reproduce the linguistic abilities of a native speaker. It tries to explain the creativity of speakers, recognises two levels of language (surface structure and 'deep' or 'underlying' structure) and sets out to explain how these levels are related.

transformations: operations that add to, delete from, substitute for or transpose sentences or parts of sentences. Transformations account for the relationship between active and passive sentences and between a sentence like 'he arrived' and the noun phrase 'his arrival'.

tree diagram: a pictorial representation of the underlying structure of a sentence. The following simplified tree diagram (also called a phrase marker) underlies all active sentences such as 'The boy ate the banana':

S → NP + VP
NP → (det) + N
VP → V + NP

velar: a consonant involving the approximation of the back of the tongue to the soft palate. The initial sounds in 'coat' and 'goat' are velars.

verb phrase: different models of grammar regard the verb phrase differently. In pre-TG models, the verb phrase referred only to the predicate in a sentence; in TG models, the verb phrase includes the predicate and all that follows it. Thus in the sentence:

He may have seen the girl on the train

TG models would call 'may have seen the girl on the train' the verb phrase.

voiced: consonants are said to be voiced when the vocal cords vibrate as the air passes through them. For instance, all the consonants in 'bad', 'good', 'knob', 'then' are voiced.

voiceless: consonants are said to be voiceless when the vocal cords do not vibrate as the air passes through them. For example, all the consonants in 'pat', 'kite', 'sip', 'thick' are voiceless.

vowel: a speech sound made while there is a free access of air through the mouth. All English vowels are voiced. The final sounds in 'tree', 'try', 'true' are vowels.

Bibliography

Our survey of linguistics offers a comprehensive coverage of the discipline. Some students will undoubtedly wish to further their knowledge and the following books will prove helpful and stimulating.

BLOOMFIELD, L.: *Language*, Henry Holt & Co., New York, 1933.

BOLINGER, D.: *Apects of Language*, Harcourt Brace Jovanovich Inc., New York, 1975.

CHOMSKY, N.: *Language and Mind*, Harcourt Brace Jovanovich Inc., New York, 1972.

CHOMSKY, N. and HALLE, M.: *The Sound Patterns of English*, Harper and Row, New York, 1968.

CRYSTAL, D.: *Prosodic Systems and Intonation in English*, Cambridge University Press, Cambridge, 1969.

CORDER, P.: *Error Analysis and Interlanguage*, Oxford University Press, London, 1981.

FILLMORE, C. J.: 'The case for case', *Universals in Linguistic Theory*, eds. E. Bach and R. Harms, Holt, Rinehart and Winston, New York, 1968.

FRIES, C. C.: *The Structure of English*, Harcourt Brace Jovanovich Inc., New York, 1952.

LEECH, G. N.: *A Linguistic Guide to English Poetry*, Longman, London, 1966.

LYONS, J.: *Semantics*, Cambridge University Press, Cambridge, 1977.

QUIRK, R. *et al*: *A Grammar of Contemporary English*, Longman, London, 1972.

SKINNER, B. F.: *Verbal Behaviour*, Appleton-Century-Crofts, New York, 1957.

STEINER, G.: *After Babel*, Cambridge University Press, Cambridge, 1974.

TODD, LORETO: *Handbook of English Grammar* (York Notes), Longman, and York Press, London, 1984.

TRAUGOTT, E. and PRATT, M. L.: *Linguistics for Students of Literature*, Harcourt Brace Jovanovich Inc., New York, 1980.

WELLS, J. C.: *Accents of English*, Cambridge University Press, Cambridge, 1982.

Index

Further titles

A DICTIONARY OF LITERARY TERMS
MARTIN GRAY

Over one thousand literary terms are dealt with in this Handbook, with definitions, explanations and examples. Entries range from general topics (comedy, epic, metre, romanticism) to more specific terms (acrostic, enjambment, malapropism, onomatopoeia) and specialist technical language (catalexis, deconstruction, *haiku*, paeon). In other words, this single, concise volume should meet the needs of anyone searching for clarification of terms found in the study of literature.

Martin Gray is Lecturer in English at the University of Stirling.

ENGLISH POETRY
CLIVE T. PROBYN

STUDYING SHAKESPEARE
MARTIN STEPHEN and PHILIP FRANKS

The author of this Handbook

LORETO TODD is a Senior Lecturer in English at the University of Leeds. Educated in Northern Ireland and Leeds she has degrees in English and Linguistics. Dr Todd has taught in England and in West Africa and has lectured in Australia, Papua New Guinea, the United States of America and the Caribbean. Her publications include ten books, among them *Pidgins and Creoles*, 1974; *Tortoise the Trickster*, 1979; *West African Pidgin Folktales*, 1979; *Variety in Contemporary English*, 1980; *Varieties of English around the World*, 1982; and *Modern Englishes*, 1984. She has written a number of articles on varieties of English, Pidgins and Creoles, folk traditions and literary stylistics. At present she is engaged in a study of the varieties and uses of spoken English. She is the author of four volumes in the York Notes Series and the York Handbook *English Grammar*.